WASHINGTON'S
Haunted Past

WASHINGTON'S

Haunted Past

Capital Ghosts of America

Pamela E. Apkarian-Russell

Haunted
America

Published by Haunted America
An Imprint of The History Press
Charleston, SC 29403
www.historypress.net

Cover Image: From his seat Lincoln can see the Potomac, Robert E. Lee's home and Arlington Cemetery. He was besieged in his presidency by those who tried to manipulate him but his honesty and common sense prevailed and have become legendary.

First published 2006

Manufactured in the United Kingdom

ISBN 1.59629.181.8

Library of Congress Cataloging-in-Publication Data

Apkarian-Russell, Pamela.
  Washington's haunted past : capital ghosts of America / Pamela E.
Apkarian-Russell.
     p. cm.
  Includes bibliographical references.
  ISBN 1-59629-181-8 (alk. paper)
  1. Ghosts--Washington (D.C.) 2. Haunted places--Washington (D.C.) I.
Title.
  BF1472.U6A65 2006
  133.109753--dc22

                         2006019578

Notice: The information in this book is true and complete to the best of our knowledge. It is offered without guarantee on the part of the author or The History Press. The author and The History Press disclaim all liability in connection with the use of this book.

In memory of my beloved brother, Dr. Robert Philip Apkarian, an internationally known and loved scientist, who was killed by a reckless motorist on February 28, 2006, while heading home on his motorcycle. His contributions to Microscopy and his generosity of spirit left our world a much better place.

In memory of Ogdah Simonian O'Gulian who gave me the opportunity to glimpse a great man.

CONTENTS

Introduction   9

America's Haunted Capital   13
The White House   17
The Octagon House   25
The Slidell House   29
The Myth and Mystery of Lincoln's Ghost   32
Ford's Theater and John Wilkes Booth   66
The Mary Surratt House   76
What a Tangled Web…   82
Lafayette Square   87
The Capitol   91
The Lincoln Memorial   103
The Library of Congress   111
Woodrow Wilson   114

Epilogue   119
Bibliography   125
About the Author   128

INTRODUCTION

My godmother Ogdah O'Gulian was supposed to be on loan from the State Department to the White House for only two weeks. She remained at the White House continuously from the Eisenhower years through the Carters', when she retired. Working for the first ladies, both Republican and Democrat, she spent a considerable amount of time in the White House itself. During her years there, she saw things that were not always of a political or human nature. She was, after all, her mother's daughter (her mother being Noonie Simonian, a seer and healer). Unlike my aunt, who only observed and didn't like to speak about it, I actively pursue and investigate the paranormal. Many limit the dimensions they delve into; I choose not to. The reason life is such a mystery is that death is an even greater and mystifying one. I find this interesting and intriguing. Perhaps that is why Washington, the District of Columbia, is such a fascinating place. Its history and shades are much more exciting because of the concentrated power, the intrigue and events that are packed into this small area. The quick and the dead still defy physics and occupy the same space. Why? We may strive to understand, and perhaps both that phenomenon and the object itself are the lesson and the answer.

On Sunday, April 27, 1969 (during the Nixon administration), I was invited to coffee and church service with the first family along with my godmother Ogdah and my Uncle Philip O'Gulian. I met the president and the first woman Marine, an elderly elegant lady whom I plied with questions. She was delightful. After the reception in the State Dining Room, Aunt Ogdah decided to attend to a few details as long as she was still "at the office," so to speak.

Abraham Lincoln felt the White House belonged to all Americans. He opened it to the public, who made a nuisance of themselves so that even the newspapers protested at the damage and vandalism, which was never kept under control. Considering the mayhem and lackadaisical security it is surprising that an assassination was not attempted in the White House itself.

Lincoln speaking to newly emancipated slaves in front of the White House. He had worked beside slaves in his youth and knew the pains and woes they suffered under slavery.

Introduction

As we walked down a corridor we stopped short as we both saw a tall man in black with a shawl or blanket around his shoulders in front of us. Moments later he disappeared before our eyes. Since that day I have dreamed of having the opportunity to investigate the White House and spend some time in the Lincoln bedroom and the other areas that are frequented by many who we only meet in history books. The poet Carl Sandburg meditated there and I would have loved to have had the opportunity to do the same.

Abe Lincoln, Abigail Adams, Andrew Jackson, Anna Surratt and others may not be "alive and well and living in the White House" but they are residents and visitors nonetheless and have been sighted by both those who believe in the supernatural and those who do not.

I feel privileged to have even received a fleeting glance of our sixteenth president, but I am greedy; I want more than just one M&M, I want an entire handful and I want them all to be green. In other words, I would like to speak with Lincoln, as I have so many questions that I would love to ask him. Teddy Roosevelt was fortunate enough to have had interactions with Lincoln all the time. However, as I shall not be allowed time to roam about the White House in search of those who have remained behind after death, it is quite exciting to take the many pieces of the puzzle and try to construct a picture. There are mysteries that perhaps a clever gumshoe could solve with today's technology and access into the files of the past. Until then you and I must peek into whatever doors have been left ajar, speculate and ponder. Sir Arthur Conan Doyle was a great believer in spiritualism. If only we had his Sherlock Holmes to help unravel the mysteries. The application of logic and perceptive analytical deduction is desperately needed on both the pro and con sides of the paranormal argument.

AMERICA'S HAUNTED CAPITAL

There are different types of ghostly manifestations and there are different reasons for paranormal activity. No one knows exactly what a ghost is and their manifestations can vary enormously. One often hears people saying that ghosts are evil, which is quite ridiculous. If a person was kindly and good in life they continue on in that manner. However, should they be miserable miscreants in life they will not change their spots when they have passed beyond the veil. Certainly, Abe Lincoln's ghost has never been evil, and he has been of great comfort and help to some presidents.

Those that are naught more than an animated memory repeat the same thing over and over without any variation, as there is not any intelligence or being regulating the manifestation. Anyone can see any type of ghost if the ghost is willing and the living being is receptive. If you place a blindfold over a person's eyes and propel them into a room and ask them to tell you what is there they cannot, unless they are daring enough or wise enough or foolish enough to remove the blindfold, or grope about in the dark and make educated guesses. The adventurous and intelligently inquisitive are those who try and solve mysteries, not deny them (the "I can't see the bottom of the ocean, therefore it doesn't exist!" syndrome). Curiosity and daring go hand in hand and sometimes a belief that one can learn or do some good is a major motivator.

Documentation of ghosts does not prove their existence, nor does lack of documentation disprove it. If you ate shish kebab last night for dinner and you tell someone about it, do they expect you to document it? If you cannot remember what you ate is it proof that you didn't? Many just feel "proof" is totally unimportant to them, as they know what they saw and felt, and

This carte de visite of Washington welcoming Lincoln to heaven shows the almost saint-like attitude attributed to the two presidents. Some have speculated that Lincoln might have been a saint or an angel sent as a guardian of the White House.

feel if people want to believe them fine and if they don't, it just isn't very important, as nothing they say or do will convince the skeptic. Too many people want or need to categorize and make rules of spectral manifestations and it just doesn't work. Every ghost is as different as every living person, as most of them were living humans once.

In my office at my old antique shop I knew exactly when the being was there, as he was interested in what I was doing on the computer. He never showed himself or answered any questions or even accepted my offer to speak with him. He was strictly fascinated with my computer. The room would go cold, the cat would scamper off into the other room and there he was peering over my shoulder at the computer. He wasn't unfriendly and why he would not or could not interact, I never could find out. There are many ghosts like this who are just passing by, curious and stopping to watch just as you would if you walked into a room where an interesting program was airing on the television. If the program is interesting it warrants a casual

The Lincoln-Douglas debates pitted the suave, sophisticated Douglas against Lincoln, the common sense, common good, no nonsense man of the people. Lincoln was drawn from the station to the debate platform by a farm wagon, while Douglas was escorted in a spiffy coach. Surprisingly, substance, truth and sincerity won the day and Lincoln the election.

or more than casual stop and look and, if not, nothing more than a fleeting glance. In Washington, there are more than a tad of interesting happenings to draw their attention. Have we not all wished to be the proverbial fly on the wall at different moments?

Many ghosts trap themselves here by having unfinished business or because they want or need to change something and feel they can still do so. There are also those who so enjoyed some place or thing so much that they find no necessity to move on to the next stage or place. These are the interesting ghosts that remain personalities and therefore are real, rather than the type that are like a film played over and over again. Washington has been filled with influential and interesting characters and it is not surprising that some of them needed or wanted to remain earthbound.

Parapsychologists say that a ghost is someone you do not know and an apparition is one you did know, such as a parent or friend. They are supposed to only come at times of great stress or impending disaster.

Personally, I feel there are those who like to drop in from time to time just to check out what we are doing.

Visions are of a religious nature and poltergeists are nasty physical manifestations almost always of a violent and destructive type. The latter two seldom enter into the history and legends of the White House and interrelated buildings. Buildings do absorb psychic vibrations, as do furniture and clothing. It is a tendency for people to return to the places they are familiar with. Tragedy draws people back as does the "home is where the heart is" places that were so dear to them in life, such as the White House rose garden for Dolley Madison. Then there are those who feel the need to stay for manifest reasons, like Abe Lincoln.

One of the most poignant lines ever written about ghosts was by Charles Dickens, who did many readings of his work in the District area as he toured around America. Marley's ghost shows Scrooge, in *The Christmas Carol*, the lost souls, some of which Scrooge recognized as people he had done business with. "The misery with them all was, clearly, that they sought to interfere, for good, in human matters, and had lost the power forever." Dickens understood the difference between ghosts and spirits, and that there are different types of ghosts, just as there are different types of people. Every ghost or manifestation must be looked at separately, as in life they were individuals with likes and dislikes, ideas, loves, hates, needs and desires. Interconnectedness, awareness, lack of awareness of each other, their plight and any goals they may have could affect the form and manifestations and who sees what and why.

Some ghosts are simply images and residues of people that once were, while others are so much more. That there are connections and even possible interactions between the Washington ghosts may be in the nature of the city itself with all of its intrigues, victories, defeats, sorrows, angers, unbending intolerance, fear and every other human emotion. High stakes have been on the table and the players are not always happy with the outcome. Some continue to play the hand but the question will always be why. People link with buildings by living in them, being in them, working in them and sometimes even dying in them.

The history behind the buildings and the happenings are our history, yours and mine, and hence we should look at them with open eyes, a critical mind and a sense of compassion. And yet there is so much mystery and intrigue that I trust you will indulge me if I cannot help but perceive it as a haunting whodunit! There are too many questions and so few answers!

THE WHITE HOUSE

The history of the White House is interwoven with the history of its
occupants and the peace and turmoil of the country. From the time of
John Adams, 1600 Pennsylvania Avenue has been home to the presidents.
However, it was George Washington, on October 13, 1792, who laid the
cornerstone on the site he had selected. This was the three hundredth
anniversary of Columbus's landing in America.

Fortunetellers have played an important part in the social and psychic
history of the White House, as have the people who have molded the design
and décor of the building as well as those who were the makers and shakers
of the nation. The home of the first families has been filled with joys and
woes just as many of the homes and buildings in the city where not only
the quick but also the dead walk. This is a glimpse into those who cannot
or will not rest in peace.

In 1799 Martha Washington visited the building designed by James
Hoban and, though she was quite pleased with it, it was Abigail Adams
who was the original first lady to reside in the building. Abigail was far
from being thrilled to occupy the White House, as it was a far cry from
what she was accustomed to in Massachusetts. Congress did not want to
allocate money for furnishing or decorating the White House and Abigail
must have found this extremely frustrating. She was forced to do without
many necessities and luxuries were heavily curtailed. After the idyllic rein
of Washington, Adams was treated rather shabbily and Abigail accepted
her lot almost stoically.

It is almost inconceivable that Abigail Adams had to hang her laundry
to dry in what is now known as the East Room, but she did. According to

Washington, D.C., The White House on a Winter's Night.

The White House at night can be a hauntingly beautiful but scary place. What haunting shadows of the past lurk around the corners?

legend, her ghost is still hanging her laundry there and she has been seen walking past with her laundry basket. She felt the building was a damp cold place. Washington at the time was very sparsely inhabited and was slightly more than a bit of smelly, damp swampland. The insects and humidity of the summer and the cold humidity of winter could not have been ideal, which gave her great cause to complain.

The East Room is also visited by troops of Civil War soldiers who camped in the room and even lit bonfires on the premises. They were supposed to be guarding the place but they were just adding to the terrible pollution of the Potomac River where the sewage ran and the typhoid spawned.

Why Mrs. Adams's ghost should be drawn to a place she couldn't wait to leave and was not fond of is a wonderment. She probably is not a true ghost but rather a manifestation of residue, actions that are repeated over and over just as if a film was playing. Abigail, a well-educated and highly cultured woman, would hardly seem the type of person to allow herself to be tied to the laundry basket for perpetuity. It is said that she leaves behind the smell of damp laundry and soap when she passes by with arms outstretched on her way to the East Room, which was the driest room in the house.

John Adams wrote to Abigail in 1774: "We live, my dear soul, in an age of trial. What will be the consequences, I know not." This can be said of every age and those who live and die in it. Certainly living in the

The White House

The East Room of the White House did not look this way when Abigail Adams resided there. It was, however, the driest room, and it was here she hung her laundry to dry. It is said her ghost, smelling of wet wash and soap, appears here.

White House was a trial for Abigail, but then again it has been for many, especially Mary Lincoln.

When John Adams moved into the White House on November 1, 1800, the building still wasn't completed. Workmen were camped all over the grounds; debris was everywhere. The damp of the winters and the almost nonexistent muddy roads were what greeted the White House's first residents. For many years the sewage ran in the streets of Washington and everyone complained about the stench of the nation's capital. For a refined woman like Abigail it must have been hell. No, it seems rather unlikely that the first lady's ghost would want to hang around, let alone hang out her laundry any longer than was necessary.

It is interesting that very little was written about the laying of the cornerstone of the White House and that the cornerstone has never been located. The only ones who celebrated this occasion with a long walk from Georgetown to the site were Peter Casanave, lodge master, and his entire lodge of Freemasons. Washington was an active master Mason and master of his lodge. The Masons were a vital part of the building of the White House. It is to be remembered that the Indians who had inspired the Sons of Liberty at the Boston Tea Party were from a Masonic lodge, many of whose members later lived in Washington.

For three hours these pseudo-Indians hauled 340 tea chests worth nine thousand English pounds and dumped them in Boston Harbor. The joke that circulated at the time was that the fish caught in the harbor after that tasted of Bohea!

On August 24, 1814, the British torched the White House. Dolley Madison, who had spent so much time decorating the White House, was one of the last to leave, as she was so intent on salvaging as much as she could of paintings, furnishings, silver and other national treasures. It is thanks to her that the Gilbert Stuart painting of George Washington is extant. How she must have hated to see all that she had worked to accomplish destroyed. (Dolley Madison and Mary Lincoln were related, both being of the Todd clan of Kentucky and both having the enviable job of decorating the White House.)

Dolley Madison made the White House into a tasteful monument and a symbol of a newly born nation. She adored the rose gardens and it is not surprising that a hundred years later, when Edith Wilson decided to redo the gardens, Dolley became so overwrought that she appeared to the gardeners waving her arms and castigating them for the sacrilege they were committing. Mrs. Wilson capitulated and had hundreds of roses planted, which more than appeased the lovely Dolley, who was used to having things her way. She remains the protector of the rose garden. Dolley's ghost is also seen at her home on Lafayette Square where she sits on the porch in her rocker watching the people go by.

The beautiful Dolley was courted by Aaron Burr before she married Madison. Unfortunately, Burr killed Alexander Hamilton in a duel and in disgrace was almost exiled out of the country until the scandal died down. When Burr was finally allowed to return to Washington he was said to have scaled a ten-foot wall to visit in secret with Dolley Payne Madison, the president's wife. Do Aaron Burr and Dolley still meet in the Octagon House garden for a secret tryst? Is there any such thing as a secret in Washington?

After the presidential residence was burned in the War of 1812, the Madisons lived for a year and a month in the Octagon House on New York Avenue, which was the home of John Tayloe. This home had been used by the French Ministry, so when the British saw the French flag flying over the building they declined to burn it. It was from here that Dolley supervised the rose garden, which was to be her legacy to future first ladies. She watched the new building rise and had a hand in refurbishing it with new items and some she had heroically saved from the conflagration.

Hoban, the original architect of the White House, rebuilt the building after the 1812 torching. Because of a violent thunderstorm that put out the fire, a segment of the sandstone walls remained standing. In September 1817 the Monroes moved into an unfinished White House.

The ghost of a British soldier who purportedly torched the White House is seen carrying that torch about the building. It is hoped that his ghost is a regretful one and not a resident pyromaniac. He was simply a soldier following orders from higher up, so how has he become linked with the building? What is his story? Regret? Remorse? We will never know.

Lincoln is the most active and important of the White House ghosts, but there are many others. Washington is as full of ghosts as it is secrets. Some are real, others are legend, while still others are fictional. Fact or fiction, often the tale is haunting.

Two first ladies, Abigail Adams and Dolley Madison, still hauntingly occupy the White House, as does Willie Lincoln, with whom his father had many conversations and twice had exhumed from his grave in order to speak to him in person.

Zachary Taylor has been seen, but infrequently. He died of gastrointestinal problems in 1850. He is one of two presidents who died in the building, and oddly enough he has not been seen anywhere near the kitchen area! Unseen but certainly heard is Andrew Jackson and his raucous laugh in the Rose Room. Mary Todd Lincoln heard that laugh but she also enjoyed listening to Thomas Jefferson play his violin. Mary felt Jefferson was an excellent musician and enjoyed listening to his solo performances.

Andrew Jackson's dying wish in 1845 was that he would meet all his friends, both white and black, on the other side. One wonders if that meant Peggy O'Neil-Eaton, too. John Eaton and Jackson were both enamored of a beautiful tavern keeper's daughter who entertained the two gentlemen graciously. It became the titillating scandal of choice, which caused problems for Jackson's administration. Jackson always said he was not fit to be president. He had a temper that reduced him to being inarticulate and was poorly thought of by Thomas Jefferson and John Quincy Adams, amongst others. Every now and then it sounds as if Jackson is entertaining Peggy again in the very bed they had romped in.

The Rose Room is also known as the Queen's Room, as no less than five queens have stayed in it. None of them have complained of Jackson's ribald laughter, though poor Queen Wilhelmina of the Netherlands had a very courteous and gentlemanly President Lincoln come knocking at her door one evening. She was flummoxed beyond words and fainted.

In the 1961 book *My Thirty Years Backstairs at the White House*, Lillian Rogers Parks tells how she was working one day all by herself in the Rose Room hemming a bedspread. Queen Elizabeth II was due to arrive on a state visit and finishing touches needed to be attended to. Suddenly the air behind

Andrew Jackson had an attempt on his life in 1835. Two pistols were fired point blank and both misfired. After they were examined it was found there was absolutely nothing wrong with either pistol. Why did they mysteriously misfire?

Lincoln

"With malice toward none, with charity toward all"

Portraits of Lincoln always show a careworn thoughtful person. It is the eyes one is drawn to.

her became exceedingly cold and she could feel someone looking over her shoulder. Even worse, she could feel the chilling pressure of a hand on the back of her chair. Filled with fear, she could not turn around but quickly placed her sewing basket on the floor and retreated posthaste. It was weeks before she could be persuaded to return to the room and then it was always when someone else was with her. Was this Jackson just being inquisitive?

The human encounters by residents and staff of this historic building are many, and some are very well documented.

Winston Churchill never mollycoddled himself, but he absolutely refused to sleep in the Lincoln bedroom. It made him more than uncomfortable; it gave him the chills and unnerved him. After a late night Churchill enjoyed a hot tub, a good cigar and some Armenian cognac. This was a productive time for him to relax and think. Getting out of the tub on one of his visits to confer with FDR during the war, he removed himself from his luxuriant long hot soak and went to get into his nightclothes in the adjoining room. Leaning against the fireplace mantel stood the late, great Mr. Lincoln. The prime minister, naked as a plucked chicken, addressed the former president. "Good evening, Mr. President, you seem to have me at an advantage." The tall lanky form was said to have smiled and vanished. Lincoln had cause to smile, just as Churchill had cause not to want to stay in that room again! It is said that he was often found across the hall in the morning, having abandoned the room. This at least is the legend that circulates about. It has also been stated that Winston Churchill would never discuss his aversion to staying in the Lincoln bedroom.

Harry Truman met Lincoln many times and even shared the office with him, indicating that he felt Lincoln had as much right there as he did. However, he never could figure out why anyone would want to return to the White House! George Washington felt much the same way and couldn't wait to end his term.

THE OCTAGON HOUSE

T he Octagon House was designed and built by Dr. William Thornton, the architect of the U.S. Capitol building. It was built as the home of John Tayloe, one of the wealthiest plantation owners of Virginia, at the suggestion of Tayloe's close friend George Washington, who felt that if he could get such an important personage to move there others would follow. After the White House was burned in the War of 1812, the Madisons lived for a year and a month in the Octagon House on New York Avenue, and it became the temporary "executive mansion."

The Treaty of Ghent, which ended the war with England, was signed on the second floor of the Octagon by Madison. This historic event was attended by John Quincy Adams and most of the important diplomats of the day. The Octagon was once the center of political and social power in Washington and the essence of that power is like perfume in the air of the building.

Until the Octagon was built, the famous Washington social season didn't exist. It was the grandeur of this home, its inhabitants and their famous and wealthy friends that propelled the growth of the District and drew others of the same ilk. There was little or nothing in the District and to have a mansion like the Octagon was a nucleus for those who were in Washington. Most congressmen and visitors were forced into staying in substandard boardinghouses so the Tayloes' hospitality was doubly welcome. It is unfortunate that Washington died before the house was finished and he never saw the completed building that he watched grow out of the swamps.

Before the Madisons had moved into the Octagon House, one of the Tayloe daughters had tragically fallen down a flight of stairs and died. After the Madisons' stay, the Tayloes returned to the Octagon House. Another

Octagon House, Washington, D. C. Built in 1798.
Occupied by President Madison when the White House was burned by the British in 1814.

The Octagon House served as the home of President and Dolley Madison after the British burned Washington in the War of 1812. This was the first important home built in Washington.

daughter, who had eloped against Tayloe's wishes, returned to reconcile with her father. In anger, he was rumored to have pushed her away and she fell down the same flight of stairs her sister had and broke her neck. Both daughters died tragically in the same manner and there are many stories of the two sisters wandering about the Octagon House, especially on the culprit stairs. But there are also stories that they died elsewhere, which is not correct. The story may have been modified in its day but the sisters did both perish on the stairs.

People have seen or think they have seen the ghostly apparitions of these two young women in the house. Does the octagonal shape of the structure account for some apparitions and paranormal activity? Probably not, though the building has experienced more activity than most in the capital. From 1855 on the building ceased to be a home and became a girls' school, an office building, an apartment house and the headquarters for the American Institute of Architects. Not until the late 1960s did the Octagon return to being a splendid mansion, and today is fully restored and a museum, where visitors can imagine the turbaned Dolley Madison entertaining two hundred of the elite in the Tayloe drawing room.

Did Dolley Madison, while living in the Octagon House, ever encounter the ghost of the first sister to fall down the spiral staircase? If she did,

The first cabinet depicts President Washington and two future presidents, John Adams and Thomas Jefferson. The image is taken from a vintage tobacco label. It has always been fashionable to use presidents and other famous people to advertise products.

nothing has ever been written of it. We do know she loved the house and loved living in it. If the first of the two Tayloe girls to die did haunt the house she did not bother the first lady, her family or guests.

The Octagon House has many mysteries about it, such as how it received its name. This beautiful Federal period building only has six sides and was designed to occupy the land shape it was to inhabit. It seems rather odd that it became known as having two more sides than it does. It is an irregular hexagon broken along the façade by a graceful semicircular bay. However, "Octagon House" is what the Tayloes named it and so it remains. In 1797, when the Octagon was beginning to be built, Tayloe and Washington, the first president of the newly united thirteen former colonies, would ride up and watch the construction of what would become the social nucleus of the area. Washington may have been retired, but was an avid watcher of the city that bore his name.

WASHINGTON'S HAUNTED PAST

Death is a dialogue between
The spirit and the dust.
"Dissolve" says Death. The Spirit, "Sir,
I have another trust."

Death doubts it, argues from the ground.
The Spirit turns away.
Just laying off for evidence,
An overcoat of clay.

Emily Dickinson, 1830–1886

Why do ghosts haunt the Octagon House? One can understand the fascination that people had for a mansion where rooms, closets doors and other stylistic features are set at odd angles. One can be seduced into fear by the stairway, with its statuary set into the walls and the twenty-two-foot chain that hangs down from above with a lantern that not only casts shadows but eerily, without cause or reason, also begins to swing as if pushed by unseen hands. The basement and kitchens also have their spine-chilling areas and accompanying noises, and even the phantom smell of cooking.

Fifteen children composed the Tayloe family, eight of whom were girls, and yet it is the two who died tragically who are still drawn to this house. Are there other ghosts in the Octagon House? Do ghosts travel from one spot to another, revisiting places dear to them and places of abhorrence? How is it that spirits become so earthbound that they are incapable, unwilling or unable to move on? Washington has many different types of hauntings and many of them are connected and interrelated because they were interrelated in real life.

THE SLIDELL HOUSE

Where the Hay-Adams Hotel stands today once was the residence of Henry Adams (1838–1918) and his wife, a building known as the Slidell House. Henry Adams's wife, Marian "Clover," was rumored to have committed suicide in the house, but there is more than a mite of justification that Henry Adams may just have murdered his wife on December 6, 1885.

There was a darkroom in the house and both Henry and Clover were amateur photographers and knew the use of potassium cyanide. Clover, a beautiful, well-educated, wealthy, intelligent woman, suffered from an upper respiratory ailment and depression over her father's recent demise. If she was suicidal and her husband Henry cared so much about her, would he not keep such chemicals locked up and would he leave her unattended at such a time?

Perhaps, after being married to a man for thirteen years who was sexually eccentric and wanted other venues, she had had enough. However, it seems from his behavior after her death that it was more likely that he wanted to go a different route.

Supposedly Henry was overwrought with grief and commissioned a sculpture by Augustus Saint-Gaudens that later became known as "Grief" as a grave marker in Rock Creek Cemetery. There are a few problems with this story, however, as Clover Adams's name is not on the memorial nor is any other information. Only after some strong-arming did the cemetery capitulate and allow this massive monument to be placed there, where for many years it was kept in shadow and darkness by the ivy and holly that surrounded it. Why did Henry try and obliterate Clover's memory from everything, including destroying her effects and personal belongings such as diaries? Guilt? Why did he not allow a stone or marker on the grave? Why did he become obsessed with the statue and so dislike the name "Grief" by which people referred to it? Whose grief?

After Clover's death Adams led a very carefree lifestyle. Did he poison his wife? Many feel that he murdered his wife so that he could have the opportunity to pursue other interests, another lifestyle. How heavily did the guilt of murder sit on Henry's conscience? He successfully got away with the deed if he did commit it but what of the matter of conscience? How could he have murdered someone who had been so good and loyal to him and had helped him so? Yet many of his contemporaries, acquaintances and friends were quite sure he had. How does one live with the knowledge one has destroyed another human being? And if he didn't murder her he certainly was instrumental in driving her to the brink of despair and providing her with the means of self-destruction. Nowhere in his autobiography does he say how he became educated in the manner and process of destroying another human being. A mere oversight? Poor Clover, poor Mrs. Adams; people referred to her as if she were a victim. Henry Adams certainly was guilty of spousal abuse and maybe it went to the final stage, murder.

"An ocean of sordidness and restless urbanity has risen over the steps of the grave, and for the first time, I suddenly ask myself whether I could endure lying there listening to that dreary vulgarity forever, and whether I could forgive myself for condemning my poor wife to it." These were the few words ever spoken by Henry Adams about Clover in all the years she had been dead, and then by a man in his seventies who was quite aware that many people thought he had killed his wife and that the house they had lived in was well noted for being haunted by Clover.

In Adams's 1918 Pulitzer Prize–winning autobiography *The Education of Henry Adams*, never once does he mention the name Marian Clover Hooper Adams. It was as if he had never been married or that she had never existed. What dark secret was he concealing and why did people hear her crying at Sixteenth and H Streets NW? Why, when the statue was commissioned, did he request that "no attempt be made to make it understandable to the human mind"? What exactly did he want not to be understood? What did Saint-Gaudens, the sculptor, think of this bizarre request? Why did he interpret it so that the statue is so desperately woeful?

Saint-Gaudens had been commissioned by Eli Bates in 1889 to sculpt the statue of Lincoln that is in the seven-acre Lincoln Park. It is considered the most lifelike image of Lincoln ever done and depicts him as he looked when he delivered the Gettysburg Address. Saint-Gaudens was a master sculptor and even designed coinage and medals. He was later involved in the Stamford White, Harry K. Thaw, Evelyn Nesbit murder and scandal that became known as the "Girl on the Red Velvet Swing." Urban legend has it that his desk was later haunted! He too had skeletons in his closet!

The "Grief" grave is purportedly haunted but by Marian Clover Adams. Anyone who looks at the statue is awed by its intense sadness, filled with morose longings. Grief oozes from the very fabric of the stone. Intense sadness overwhelms people and some feel faint while contemplating the statue. Is this a case of a haunting or of a master artist having breathed emotion and life into his creation? And what of the veiled figure who is sometimes seen there?

Is the haunting that of a woman who felt her self-esteem so low because of her husband's inability or lack of sexual desire in her gender to grieve? Or is Clover overwhelmed with frustration and sadness that Henry "got rid of her"?

The confusion over the identity of the resident spirit in the Slidell House itself is simply a case of two women with the same last name melding into one person. Abigail Adams, being the better known of the two, was incorrectly identified as the ghost despite the fact that she was hardly the type of woman to be overwhelmed by grief. Urban legends are difficult to iron back into the fabric of truth. Henry Adams moved into the Slidell House in 1877 and Abigail Adams, his ancestor, never saw it. Then again, poor Clover never was to see the new house she and Henry were building and she was set to be mistress of the manor of, so to speak. The Slidell House was torn down in 1922 and the U.S. Chamber of Commerce was erected in its place.

Was Henry Adams the reason his wife haunts her old residence and tomb? And why doesn't Henry's ghost walk and mourn in front of the unmarked slab he condemned his wife to lie beneath—since he obsessively spent so much time in front of it during his lifetime, why not in death? Or does he?

> *The silver swan, who living had no note,*
> *When death approached unlocked her silent throat;*
> *Leaning her breast against the reedy shore,*
> *Thus sung her first and last, and sung no more.*
> *Farewell, all joys; o death, come close my eyes;*
> *More geese than swan now live, more fools than wise.*
>
> *Orlando Gibbons*

THE MYTH AND MYSTERY OF LINCOLN'S GHOST

If Lincoln was the heart, soul and conscience of the nation and he has been masterfully denied justice, how can we the people not be restless also? Just as the controversy of the Kennedy assassination continues, so does that of Lincoln. Masking these national tragedies breeds mistrust that festers. Lincoln said, "The worst thing you can do for those you love is to do for them the things they could or should do for themselves." Today his ghost is obviously trying desperately to uncover the mystery of his murder but may need assistance from those who live in the house he gravitates to. Sometimes even the best of us need assistance.

It has often been remarked by current and past occupants of the White House that it is unwise to publicly discuss ghosts or spectral visitors lest others think one mad. Both Mary and Abe Lincoln did discuss the paranormal and it was widely written about in European newspapers. There was a great revival of spiritualism in Lincoln's time, which might have been because of the war.

In the 1850s the spiritualist movement was very much in vogue and was socially accepted as valid as well as fashionable. Queen Victoria dressed in black after Albert, the Prince Consort, passed away in 1861 and went into mourning for the remainder of her life. When Mr. Brown, her gillie, passed away she carried the mourning to a deeper level of grief, if that was possible, as she had already been dubbed the widow of Windsor! Mr. Brown was a sensitive who was able to contact the dead and was the Queen's closest friend and confidant. When Mr. Brown passed away Queen Victoria was beside herself with grief. First she lost Albert and then Mr. Brown—it was unbearable and she was inconsolable.

Mourning became very fashionable in Victorian England. In Charles Dickens's *Dombey and Sons* Mrs. Pipchin's mourning attire is described as thus: "black bombazine, of such a lusterless, deep, dead, somber shade, that gas itself couldn't light her up after dark, and her presence was a quencher, to any number of candles." Victoria was only one year younger than Mary Todd Lincoln but she left a great influence on her society as well as fashion. Widows' weeds, as the crepe and bombazine dresses were called, were inflicted by society of their age, as is most fashion.

In Washington before, during and after the Civil War photographers were very active. It wasn't just Matthew Brady who went out onto the battlefield to take photographs of the multitude of deceased soldiers. Most of the time photographs were taken prior to the soldier leaving for the battlefield. If he died the negative was reprinted with a black mourning border to be given to friends and family, a memorial of their sacrifice for the country and their bravery. There were very strict regulations on the decorum of mourning protocol and it was offensive to both society and the church if pious resignation to the teachings of the church and God were flouted. The Victorians were not a flamboyant group on the whole and restraint and proper decorum were the order of the day.

"In Memoriam" cards were given at funerals to the attendees and then sent to those who could not be there. The Victorian era was one that glorified mourning. Certainly, it was an era in which our country had much to mourn. These cards may have lost their popularity after Victoria's day, but they are widely collected, as are the actual photographic ones that were done with the deceased on the front and on the reverse an ornate mourning picture such as this.

Memorial art and jewelry became the rage. Memento mori were exchanged and even collected. One of the fashions of the day became hair wreaths and jewelry. This reached a high art form with the hair of the deceased and the hair of friends and relatives woven to make elaborate memorial confections to hang on the wall or place in lockets to wear in order to keep the presence of the departed with one in perpetuity. These items are prized today for their artistic quality and beauty but in Victoria's and Mary Lincoln's day they were also focus points, links to the deceased that spiritualists and seers could use to contact them. Just as a crystal ball acts as a magnet to induce contact, the hair, a once living part of the person, was a link. What would make that link even stronger was to take the hair of the mourners and bury it with their loved ones. It was also so that the deceased did not forget them and perhaps would return with comfort and hope for the living.

President Lincoln was a great believer in the paranormal and actively pursued it; he was quite likely a gifted seer. A piece of sheet music called "The Dark Séance Polka" appeared in England, depicting Lincoln in a darkened room holding a candle. Fiddles and tambourines prance about in the air surrounding him, while spiritualists dance about in merry abandonment. The caption read "Abraham Lincoln & the Spiritualists." From the 1850s on many books were written on the subject and ephemera, such as sheet music, almanacs and cards, were abundant in America as well as England and Europe.

There are so many stories of Lincoln relating to spiritualists, séances and the paranormal that one could produce an anthology of just them. Lincoln was said to consult spiritualists in order to receive more in-depth information about what was happening on the war front and what was going to occur in the hours and days ahead. A War Department document relates how Lincoln rushed down to the telegraph room and sent a message that a certain Confederate sector would break through the ranks at a certain place and it must be stopped as it would make all the difference if the Union won or lost the battle. The information was acted upon and because of it the battle was won. Perhaps the battle would have been won anyway but what if Lincoln had not sent the message? He quite often sent information that he had received from psychics and spiritualists. He often sent messages to generals regarding information that he had no way of knowing but was pertinent and helpful to the generals who received the information.

It would seem that Lincoln felt that he left much undone, and to atone for that he needed to try and guide those who would fulfill the office of president in a manner he thought proper. Almost every president since has had to deal with Lincoln's presence and manifestations. Lincoln, marked and scarred by many tragedies in his life, not withstanding the terrible manner of his death, used mediums and felt during his lifetime that he could communicate with the beyond. During World War II manifestations of Lincoln were profuse, especially in the map room. If the man had premonitions and visions while he was alive and was so utterly committed to the preservation of the country, would he not try to help, control or intervene after his body had died, especially if he felt that things were not on the right track? No wonder so many people are reluctant or refuse to speak about spectral incidents in the White House.

The Empress Eugenie, wife of Napoleon III, used the services of Madam Blavatsky, who was perhaps the greatest spiritualist of her time. Though Empress Eugenie and Queen Victoria lived far from the Potomac, news and information was rapidly spread throughout the world via newspapers and the massive amount of letters that were written. Therefore, a very global hotline was already disseminating lachrymose, overtly sweet and flowery worded memorials. Mary Todd and Abraham Lincoln were very aware of all these when their second son, Willie, passed on.

They were both heartbroken and they had both read the book *East Lynne* by Ellen Price Wood, which tells of a dying child and his seeing the pearly gates and Jesus coming to take him away. Angels surrounding the bed of a dying child became very popular print motifs to hang in the home, especially in children's rooms, but why? Was it comforting for the child who certainly knew how many of his peers around him never made it to adulthood? The concept of angels protecting one's child when one no longer could certainly may have been comforting to adults.

When Willie Lincoln died, unconscious from internal bleeding and typhoid, he was medically treated the way anyone one else of that era would and hence he joined the ranks of thousands who died from the dreaded disease. Shortly after Willie passed on it became popular to take photographs of dead children and people in their coffins. Perhaps just having a photograph of poor Willie in death would have assuaged the Lincolns' grief somewhat. Willie died at age eleven in February of 1862 and it was just another tremor to the slightly unstable emotional constitution of Mary Lincoln.

It has often been written that Abe and Mary had a very stormy relationship; however, it also seems that they were devoted to one another and that Mary cared deeply for her husband. Her meddling into government business was minor and it seems the major contention was her inability to manage money and stay within her budget, which drove

Lincoln loved to have his family around him and to read aloud to them. Photos like this were very much in vogue at the time. Queen Victoria had quite a mania for collecting these and she hired agents to purchase cards of famous people for her collection. Lincoln's portraits were among them.

Lincoln is here crowned with a laurel because he was not only the victor, if there was such a thing as a victor when so many had died, but because he too was sacrificed to the god of war. To Lincoln, victory was unification.

THOMAS JEFFERSON

Third President of
The United States.
Born April 2, 1743.
Inaugurated 1801 and 1805.
Died July 4, 1826.

Mark Twain said that "greatness was the ability to gain recognition." It is perplexing, then, that Thomas Jefferson, who wrote the Declaration of Independence, was the third president of the United States, was the founding father of the Library of Congress and was one of the greatest Renaissance men this country has ever known, is often forgotten when considering the founding of this country. If great means rich, like some think, then Jefferson was not great; but if it regards his contribution in time, thought, ideas and loyalty, rank him among the greatest men who ever lived in America.

There were possibly as many as eight séances held in the White House. It is said that Lincoln accepted gifts and read books and letters from mediums, but never became a believer. According to *Lincoln Day By Day*, edited by Earl Schenck Miers, the president "allegedly attended a spiritualist séance in the White House" as late as April 23, 1863.

Lincoln to distraction. Thomas Jefferson once said, "Never spend your money before you have it." But Lincoln was unable to impress this on Mary. Money seemed to be a recurring problem in other administrations as well, but then that is not unique to first families of the nation either.

When it came to personal tragedies, the Lincolns were average in an era when so many mothers died in childbirth and so many children died of diseases that today are easily eradicated or cured. Medicine and science have progressed and changed so much since Lincoln's time that the doctors of Lincoln's day hardly resemble the doctors we have today.

For example, as Lincoln lay dying in the Petersen Boarding House just across the street from Ford's Theater, he bled to death and the crowd that surrounded him was more interested in taking souvenir bandages soaked in his blood than affecting any cure, let alone easing his suffering. The undertaker and the makers of crepe buntings to drape buildings and trains seemed more important than saving the life of the president or easing his pain. In all likelihood they didn't have a hope of saving him, but they need not have made him suffer any more than he had to. Sanitary conditions were nonexistent and Lincoln must have suffered greatly.

Lincoln's precognitive dream about his own untimely death is well documented because he related the dream to his close friend Ward Hill Lamon.

> *About ten days ago, I retired very late. I soon began to dream. There seemed to be a death-like stillness about me. Then I heard subdued sobs, as if a number of people were weeping. I thought I left my bed and wandered downstairs. There the silence was broken by the same pitiful sobbing, but the mourners were invisible. I went from room to room. No living person was in sight, but the same mournful sounds met me as I passed alone. I was puzzled and alarmed. Determined to find the cause of a state of things so mysterious and shocking, I kept on until I arrived at the East Room. Before me was a catafalque on which rested a corpse wrapped in funeral vestments. Around it were stationed soldiers who were acting as guards; and there was a throng of people, some gazing mournfully upon the corpse, whose face was covered, others weeping pitifully. "Who is dead in the White House?" I demanded of one of the soldiers. "The president, he was killed by an assassin."*

Are the ghosts of the Civil War era more romantic or appealing to us because of the trauma and longevity of the conflict? If there had not been an assassination, and John Wilkes Booth had not become a semi-heroic villain-hero and poor Mary Surratt's family gathered into the tragedy, would this conflict to preserve *e pluribus unum* have captured the imaginations of writers, poets, historians and Americans from all walks of life today?

> *I walked down the garden walk*
> *To bid my love good-by,*
> *And as I passed the rose's stalk*
> *What should my eyes espy*
> *But, nestled like a brooding dove*
> *In some sequestered spot,*
> *The very thing I told my love—*
> *A dear (FORGET-ME-NOT)!*
> *I stooped and plucked the little flower.*
> *He said, "What do you seek?"*
> *I answered, "In the twilight hour*
> *Let this love for me speak!"*
> *I twined it softly in his vest,*
> *His arms were round me felled—*
> *And as I leaned upon his breast*
> *He said I was his world!*
> *His sword was girt upon his thigh,*
> *His plume waved in the breeze;*
> *And all the twilight seemed to sigh*
> *Among the garden trees!*
> *I looked into his eyes and felt*
> *As happy maidens feel,*
> *When two loving spirits melt*
> *In one for woe or weal.*
> *He drew me closer to his heart,*
> *My hand was on his breast;*
> *He said, "My love! Though now we part,*
> *This heart can never rest*
> *Until I bring you back your flower*
> *And claim, where now we stand,*
> *In some sweet, future twilight hour,*
> *This darling little hand!"*
> *These were the words I heard him say—*
> *The last I ever heard!*
> *I saw him slowly ride away*
> *While not a step I stirred.*
> *I could not move—I saw him turn*
> *And kiss his hand to me.*

Ah, how my spirit then did yearn
For what should never be.
This little casket that I wear
The rest can better tell—
A withered flower, a lock of hair,
A blood stained word, "Farewell!"
They buried him upon the field,
Upon the battle plain;
And life to me can never yield
A comfort to my pain
I often at the twilight hour,
Steal down the garden walk,
Where once I plucked the little flower
Beneath the rose's stalk;
And when I reach the wicker-gate,
And no one else is nigh,
I almost think I see him wait,
As then to say "Good-by."
And sometimes when the shadows creep
Along the garden wall
I hear a voice that makes me weep
Out of the darkness call.
It seems to say as still I stand
Upon the same old spot—
"I'm waiting for that little hand—
my dear, FORGET-ME-NOT!"

This poem appeared in *Harpers Weekly* on February 27, 1864, and not only is representative of the sentimentality of the time but also shows that death was everywhere, from the home to the battlefield. Women died in record numbers giving birth; children died of diseases; consumption, typhoid, cholera, diphtheria and gangrene waged war upon all humanity, while the battlefield left carnage for the carrion feeders. Desperate for comfort, it was only natural that people should grasp at anything that would give them hope or faith. Contact with the deceased through spiritualism was one of these outlets and literature was another. It was during this era that Charles Dickens's works were being published weekly, chapter by chapter in the newspapers and periodicals, and he gave readings and lectures. Hope was all that many had.

How many men lay on the battlefield and died from lack of medical care? Violent deaths often act as gravity to spirits, keeping them from rising on to the next level or plane.

The Blue and the Gray

No more shall the war-cry sever,
Or the winding rivers be red;
They banish our anger forever
When they laurel the graves of the dead!
Under the sod and the dew,
Waiting the Judgment Day:
Love and tears for the Blue,
Tears and love for the Gray.

Francis Miles Finch (1827–1907)

Fragile as the petals of a rose was life in the Victorian era and nowhere was this more evident than in the White House during the Lincoln administration. Two of Lincoln's sons had died, friends had passed on in the battlefields, Lincoln had lost his first love Ann Rutledge and every day he received dispatches telling of the thousands dying on the battlefield and of those that could have been saved if there had been sufficient doctors and supplies. Life was pretty much like the children's nursery rhyme "Who Killed Cock Robin?" All participate and then the bell rings. "Ask not for whom the bell tolls for it tolls for you." If Lincoln was morose he had a right to be, as it seemed inevitable that assassination should be his doom.

Lincoln may not have been a spiritualist but he was extremely knowledgeable about spiritualism, having read many books and having corresponded with some of the well-known spiritualists of the day. There were some well-known Georgetown mediums known as the Lauries and Mary Lincoln certainly visited them many times in order to contact Eddie and Willie, her two departed children.

There were as many as eight séances in the White House and it is inconceivable, knowing Lincoln's interest and Mary's need to contact the children, that the president wouldn't have participated in a good many of them. The following account, however, was probably a hoax. It was probably someone making fun of both spiritualism and the Lincolns' belief in it. Shockle, the medium, has never been mentioned anywhere as existing. Nor during the era did any of the supposed participants report on or write about it.

Washington, April 23, 1863. A few evenings since Abraham Lincoln,
president of the United States, was induced to give a spiritual soiree

The Myth and Mystery of Lincoln's Ghost

The Lincoln Memorial is a magnet that draws people of all countries and of every ethic group and religious denomination. It inspires and gives hope to millions. Lincoln's statue seems to breathe and speak to those who are disenfranchised and need hope. It seems amazing that Lincoln once fought a duel using a saber when he was living in Illinois. Neither man was injured. There were many sides to Lincoln's personality and wisdom including humor and wit.

in the crimson room at the White House, to test the wonderful alleged supernatural powers of Mr. Charles E. Shockle. It was my good fortune, as a friend of the medium, to be present, the party consisting of the President, Mrs. Lincoln, Mr. Welles, Mr. Stanton, Mr. L—, of New York, and Mr. F—, of Philadelphia. We took our seats in the circle about 8 o'clock, but the President was called away shortly after the manifestations commenced, and the spirits, which had apparently assembled to convince him of the power, gave visible tokens of their displeasure at the President's absence, by pinching Mr. Stanton's ears and twitching Mr. Welles's beard. He soon returned, but it was some time before harmony was restored, for the mishaps to the secretaries caused such bursts of laughter that the influence was very unpropitious. For some half hour the demonstrations were of a physical character—tables were moved and the picture of Henry Clay, which hangs on the wall, was swayed more than a foot, and two candelabras, presented to President Adams, were twice raised nearly to the ceiling. It was nearly 9 o'clock before Shockle was fully under spiritual influence, and so powerful were the subsequent manifestations that twice during the evening restoratives were applied, for he was much weakened; and though I took no notes,

I shall endeavor to give you as faithful an account as possible of what took place. Loud rappings about 9 o'clock were heard directly beneath the President's feet, and Mr. Shockle stated that an Indian desired to communicate. "Well, sir," said the President, "I should be happy to hear what his Indian majesty has to say. We have recently had a visitation from our red brethren, and it was the only delegation, black, white, or blue which did not volunteer some advice about the conduct of the war." The medium then called for pencil and paper, and they were laid upon the table, in sight of all. A handkerchief was then taken from Mr. Stanton, and the materials were carefully concealed from sight. In less space of time than it has required me to write this, knocks were heard and the paper was uncovered. To the surprise of all present it read as follows: "Haste makes waste, but delays cause vexations. Give vitality by energy. Use every means to subdue. Proclamations are useless; make a bold front and fight the enemy; leave traitors at home to the care of loyal men. Less note of preparation, less parade and policy-talk, more action. HENRY KNOX." "That is not Indian talk, Mr. Shockle," said the President. "Who is Henry Knox?" I suggested to the medium to ask who General Knox was, and before the words were from my lips the medium spoke in a strange voice: "The first Secretary of War." "Oh, yes, General Knox," said the President, who, turning to the Secretary, said: "Stanton that message is for you; it is from your predecessor." Mr. Stanton made no reply. "I should like to ask General Knox," said the President, "if it is within the scope of his ability to tell us when the rebellion will be put down." In the same manner as before his message was received: "Washington, Lafayette, Franklin, Wilberforce, Napoleon, and myself have held frequent consultations upon this point. There is something which our spiritual eyes cannot detect which appear well formed. Evil has come at times by removal of men from high positions, and there are those in retirement whose abilities should be made useful to hasten the end. Napoleon says concentrate your forces upon one point; Lafayette thinks that the rebellion will die of exhaustion; Franklin sees the end approaching, as the South must give up for want of mechanical ability to compete against Northern mechanics. Wilberforce sees hope only in a negro army."—KNOX.

"Well," exclaimed the President, "opinions differ among the saints as well as among the sinners. They don't seem to understand running the machines among the celestials much better than we do. Their talk and advice sound very much like the talk of my cabinet—don't you think so, Mr. Welles?" "Well, I don't know—I will think the matter over and see what conclusion to arrive at." Heavy raps were heard and

the alphabet was called for, when "That's what's the matter" was spelt out. There was a shout of laughter, and Mr. Welles stroked his beard. "That means, Mr. Welles," said the President, "that you are apt to be long-winded, and think the nearest way home is the longest way round. Short cuts in war times. I wish the spirits could tell us how to catch the Alabama." The lights, which had been partially lowered, almost instantaneously became so dim that I could not see sufficiently to distinguish the features of any one in the room, and on the large mirror over the mantel-piece there appeared the most beautiful though supernatural picture ever beheld. It represented a sea view, the Alabama with all steam up flying from the pursuit of another large steamer. Two merchantmen in the distance were seen partially destroyed by fire. The picture changed, and the Alabama was seen at anchor under the shadow of an English fort—from which an English flag was waving. The Alabama was floating idly, not a soul on board, and no signs of life visible about her. The picture vanished, and in letters of purple appeared, "The English people demanded this of England's aristocracy." "So England is to seize the Alabama finally?" said the President. "It may be possible; but Mr. Welles, don't let one gunboat or monitor less be built." The spirits called for the alphabet, and again, "That's what's the matter," was spelt out. "I see, I see," said the President. "Mother England thinks that what's sauce for the goose may be sauce for the gander. It may be tit, tat, too, hereafter. But it is not very complimentary to our navy, anyhow." "We've done our best, Mr. President," said Mr. Welles. "I'm maturing a plan which, when perfected, I think, if it works well, will be a perfect trap for the Alabama." "Well, Mr. Shockle," remarked the President, "I have seen strange things and heard rather odd remarks, but nothing which convinces me, except the pictures, that there is anything very heavenly about all this. I should like, if possible, to hear what Judge Douglas says about this war." "I'll try to get his spirit," said Mr. Shockle, "but it sometimes happens, as it did tonight in the case of the Indian, that though first impressed by one spirit, I yield to another more powerful. If perfect silence is maintained I will see if we cannot induce General Knox to send for Mr. Douglas." Three raps were given, signifying assent to the proposition. Perfect silence was maintained, and after an interval of perhaps three minutes, Mr. Shockle rose quickly from his chair and stood up behind it, resting his left arm on the back, his right thrust into his bosom. In a voice such as no one could mistake who had ever heard Mr. Douglas, he spoke. I shall not pretend to quote the language. It was eloquent and choice. He urged the President to throw aside all advisers *who hesitate about the policy to be pursued, and to listen to the wishes of the people, who would sustain him at all points if his aim was, as he believed it was, to restore the Union. He said their [sic] were Burrs and Blennerhassetts living, but that they would wither before the popular approval which would follow one or two victories, such as he thought must take place ere long. The turning point in this war will be the proper use of these victories—if wicked men in the first hours of success think it time to devote their attention to party, the war will be prolonged; but if victory is followed up by energetic action, all will be well. "I believe that," said the President, "whether it comes from spirit or human." Mr. Shockle was much prostrated after this, and at Mrs. Lincoln's request it was thought best to adjourn the dance [sic—séance?], which, if resumed, I shall give you an account of. Yours, as ever. MELTON.*

Spiritualists warned Lincoln repeatedly before the assassination of a terrible conspiracy against his life and of his death. Both he and Mary were convinced it would be soon after the election and he was even specifically warned not to go to the theater.

On Good Friday, April 14, 1865, only eight days after the South surrendered, a reluctant Abe Lincoln agreed to go to Ford's Theater, where

The emancipation of the slaves was one of Lincoln's goals. An abolitionist at heart, Lincoln was very upset with John Brown and the Harper's Ferry incident as it meant that war would be inevitable and he could do nothing to preserve the Union without bloodshed.

Our American Cousin, a comedy, was playing. When he left the White House on that fatal evening to attend Ford's Theater he was extremely morose and the guard pleaded with him not to go. Lincoln, who always just said "goodnight" to the guard, said "goodbye" that evening. He was cognizant that he was on his way to his death. But, like many before him and since, he ignored the warnings and premonitions, and John Wilkes Booth moved from the realm of one of the great actors of his generation to that of political assassin.

It is interesting that as Lincoln sat in his box chatting with Mary and their guests they were discussing the Holy Land and his last words were, "There is no place I wish to see more than Jer——" He never finished the word Jerusalem, as that is when John Wilkes Booth shot him point blank in the back of the head.

There are so many reasons that Lincoln would maintain a presence in the White House; one might be that all the rumors and controversy about the supposed death of Booth and that the conspiracy against Lincoln and his Cabinet are more than half true. Besides still wanting to lead the country in the direction he felt it should go, it could be that Lincoln is still trying to finish the puzzle and bring the truth of what really happened into the light.

The evening that Lincoln was shot at the Ford Theater, the comedy playing was "Her American Cousin" starring Laura Keene. Lincoln enjoyed the theater and attended many of the Washington theaters to relax and momentarily wash away the cares of the presidency.

LINCOLN CENTENNIAL
SOUVENIR

1809

1909

ABRAHAM LINCOLN
THE MARTYRED PRESIDENT.

From the humblest origin, by zeal and personal worth,
he reached the highest pinnacle of fame.
His name will ever shine pre-eminently in
history as the Champion of Liberty.

Many presidents were not born with the proverbial silver spoon in their mouths and had to work at menial low-paying jobs as well as school themselves. These self-made men like Lincoln understood and cared about the people, knew their limits and their capacities and always tried to raise people to a higher level.

The Myth and Mystery of Lincoln's Ghost

O Captain! My Captain!

O Captain! my Captain! Our fearful trip is done;
The ship has weather'd every rack, the prize we sought is won;
The port is near, the bells I hear, the people all exulting,
While follow eyes the steady keel, the vessel grim and daring;
But O heart! Heart! Heart!
O the bleeding drops of red,
Where on the deck my Captain lies,
Fallen cold and dead.

O Captain! my Captain! Rise up and hear the bells;
Rise up—for you the flag is flung—for you the bugle trills;
For you bouquets and ribboned wreaths—for you the shores a-crowding
For you they call, the swaying mass, their eager faces turning
Here Captain! Dear father!
This arm beneath your head;
It is some dream than on the deck,
You've fallen cold and dead.

My Captain does not answer, his lips are pale and still;
My father does not feel my arm, he has no pulse nor will;
The ship is anchor'd safe and sound, its voyage closed and done
From fearful trip, the victor ship comes in with object won;
Exult, o shores, and ring, o bells!
But I, with mournful tread,
Walk the deck my captain lies,
Fallen cold and dead.

Walt Whitman

Walt Whitman was in the audience at Ford's Theater the night that Lincoln died and was a great admirer of his. He wrote this poem as a memoriam.

The conspiracy story and cover-up surrounding Lincoln's assassination seem to have even more validity than those of John F. Kennedy's assassination, which has numerous similarities. The myth and mystery are important to consider in order to try and understand why Lincoln's ghost is seen so often and by so many. Is he frustrated that after all these years the government has not even tried to uncover the mystery of his death? To begin with,

Booth's family, almost all in the acting community and totally uninvolved in the assassination, swear that the person killed in Richard Garrett's barn on the morning of April 26, 1865, was definitely not John Wilkes Booth. Who would know better than his family? Why was Booth's diary impounded by Secretary of War Stanton for two years after the purported death and when it was released, why were eighteen pages missing? Where did those pages go, where are they now and why were they removed from the diary? Was Stanton the culprit? Did he remove the pages because they implicated him? What of the theory that the diary that was later released was not the one confiscated, but a forged document?

How is it that after the assassination, from California to England to Europe, John Wilkes Booth was spotted all over (minus the mustache) by people who recognized him or knew him? His own mother said she saw him in San Francisco in 1866 and he explained to her how he was able to escape. How is it that Booth's supposed corpse was never properly identified by anyone and rushed out of Caroline County, where he was supposedly killed, and secretly buried? And was he or the substitute body buried in Washington? How much of his act was for patriotic reasons and how much was for fame and glory and monetary remuneration?

A gypsy fortuneteller once told Booth, according to legend and his sister Asia, as she reported in *The Unlocked Book*, "You have a bad hand, the lines all cris-cras! It's full enough of sorrow—full of trouble—trouble in plenty. You will break many hearts but they will mean nothing to you. You will die young and many will mourn you. You will make a bad end and have plenty to love you. You'll have a fast life—short, but a grand one…Young sir, I've never seen a worse hand and I wish I had not seen it, but if I were a girl I would follow you through the world for your handsome face."

Yes, Booth was very handsome, elegant, cultured, passionate and a talented actor, but he was not content to be just the toast of the town. He wanted so much more…to become a legend. He was ruthless.

Not one person of impeccable reputation or who knew Booth intimately could, would or did say that the person killed in the burning barn was Booth or if the person had killed himself or had been killed by the soldiers. There were many that would definitely say that the man who died, whom Sergeant Boston Corbett said he killed, was not Booth and that Corbett was delusional, heard and spoke to God all the time and was considered crazy by those who knew him. He shot Booth because God's angels told him to do it.

Corbett was known as the Mad Hatter because he had been a hat cleaner by trade. His orders were that Booth should be taken alive, yet he fired a lone bullet that hit Booth in the back of the head—in the same area that

Lincoln had been shot. Booth was then dragged out of the burning barn to the steps of the Garrett farmhouse where Lucinda Holloway cradled his head in her lap until he died. She cut off a lock of the dead man's hair; but was it Booth's? He certainly could not have committed suicide as the person killed in that barn was shot in the back of the head. If Corbett was part of the cover-up it might have been his job to make sure there was a body to pass off as Booth's. Dead men don't talk and can't give away secrets!

All of the secrecy and bizarre behavior that followed reek of a cover-up. If you were Lincoln and you knew this had happened wouldn't you be upset and want the truth to be told? Lincoln was known as Honest Abe, after all. If he spent his entire life telling the truth, why shouldn't the truth be told about his death and those responsible for murdering him? Could the ghost of Lincoln still be waiting for justice before he is allowed or allows himself to rest in peace? Why does the plot become thicker and the circles of conspirators grow larger? Is there such a thing as a peaceful grave for Lincoln?

> *And in the narrow house o' death*
> *Let winter round me rave;*
> *And the next flow'rs deck the spring*
> *Bloom on my peaceful grave!*
>
> *Dread Omnipotence, alone*
> *Can heal the wound, he gave;*
> *Can point the brimful grief-worn eyes*
> *To scenes behind the grave.*
>
> *Robert (Robbie) Burns, 1791*

It is unfortunate that so many people were tragically involved in Lincoln's demise. Mary Todd Lincoln grieved herself into insanity so that her son Robert had no choice but to have her committed to an asylum. Her son Tad, retuning with her from Europe to England, caught a chill and died of consumption.

Major Rathbone and Miss Harris were guests in the presidential box the night of the assassination. They later married but it was a short and tragic union, as he committed suicide after murdering her. The only reason their children were not also murdered was that the nurse in charge of the children, Inzola and Alonso, removed them from harm's way.

All nine of the officers who composed the commission that condemned Mary Surratt died tragic deaths, many by suicide.

Lincoln always knew he was to be the sacrificial lamb. Liberty with her sword could honor him but not save him from his kismet.

The Myth and Mystery of Lincoln's Ghost

Louis Weichman said he lived in fear of the ghost of Booth for having been a witness against Mary Surratt. Was this just a guilty conscience mixed with a vivid imagination? In all likelihood, Weichman prefabricated much of his testimony and used it to his own benefit in order to obtain notoriety and monetary gain. Mary Surratt, if she had been a vengeful ghost, should have gone after him for his prevarications!

Again the silent wheel of time
Their annual round have driv'n,
And you, tho' scarce in maiden prime,
Are so much nearer Heav'n.

Robert (Robbie) Burns, January 1, 1787

It seems that Mary Surratt was closer to heaven than those who tried her and testified against her; or even those who, when she begged, "Please don't let me fall" (the trap door on the gallows was removed from under the person's feet), did not have mercy or justice in their thoughts and actions.

The controversy, the mystery, the intrigue, the many strata of interconnecting causes and effects have as their nucleus Abraham Lincoln, who is the most active in an incredible cast of characters. If the play continues on, and it does not seem that there has been any ebbing in the sightings and ghostly activities, then there must be a cause. Is this why so many occupants of the White House have had séances in order to find out exactly what Mr. Lincoln wants and how to achieve it? How thick is the intrigue surrounding the cover-up about the first presidential assassination in America?

Three quotes from Lincoln provide insight into the man and his psyche:

I do the very best I know how, the very best I can, and I mean to keep doing so 'till the end. If the end brings me out all right, what is said against me won't amount to anything.

Whenever any church will inscribe over its altar, as its sole qualification for membership, the Savior's condensed statement of the substance of both the law and Gospel, Thou shalt love the Lord thy God with all thy heart and with all thy soul, and with all thy mind, and thy neighbor as thyself, that church I will join with all my heart, and all my soul.

I do not pretend to be a prophet. But though not a prophet, I see a very dark cloud on the horizon. That dark cloud is coming from Rome. It is filled with tears of blood. It will rise and increase till its flanks will be torn by a flash of lightning, followed by a fearful peal of thunder. Then a cyclone, such as the world has never seen will pass over the country, spreading ruin and desolation from north to south. After it is over, there will be long days of peace and prosperity; for popery, with its Jesuits and merciless Inquisition will have been forever swept away from our country. Neither I nor you, but our children will see these things.

Lincoln was able to prophesize and in it was his fear of holy inquisitions, which would destroy tolerance and understanding. He may not have been another Nostradamus but he did have visions and left warnings in his writings and speeches. Though incredibly accepting, he would not stand for intolerance and justly feared the book burners of the world.

"I want it said of me that I always plucked a thistle and planted a flower when I thought a flower would grow," said Lincoln.

Mary Lincoln was a victim of her times and the fact that she resided in the White House. From the moment she arrived Washington society had decided that she was a country bumpkin and of little consequence. No matter what she did it was never good enough. The fact that she was not a handsome woman was held against her. She came from a good family in Kentucky and was well educated in Southern hospitality, so she had style and taste even if Washingtonians didn't want to accept it.

Much of Washington society was from Virginia and Maryland and these old families were often sympathetic to the South. Many of these first families of high society headed home and shunned the "court of the black Republican queen." She was in a no-win position. Before Willie died Mary was able to garner some support but afterward, no matter what she said or did, it was misconstrued and misinterpreted. Sometimes her actions and words were open to question. The Southerners took every opportunity to make fun of her and rip her apart. The Northerners thought she was a Southern spy and was smuggling information out of the White House to the South, as her brothers were in the Confederate army. Samuel and Alexander Todd were both killed during the war fighting for the Confederacy. Almost all of her family supported or fought for the Confederacy. She was in a compromised position and though she loved her family dearly her allegiances were to the Union her husband was fighting to preserve. Lincoln actually had to appear in front of a Congressional investigating committee to assure the committee his wife was not a spy for the Confederacy and was loyal to the Union. This must have been both humiliating and painful for both the president and Mary, but rumors were rampant and had to be staunched. Mary once said, "Why should I sympathize with the rebels? They would hang my husband

Mary Todd Lincoln in her inaugural dress. She was an elegant dresser and indulged her wardrobe further than the president's budget would allow. This was a high point of contention.

tomorrow if it was in their power, and perhaps gibbet me with him. How then can I sympathize with a people that are at war with me and mine?" She always tried to put her best foot forward even though she knew it would do her no good. She remarked to White House Secretary W.O. Stoddard that she was prepared to do her duty, "while her smiling guests pulled her to pieces." Her dinners, parties and banquets met with some success, but even with her best foot forward and a White House she had been allotted $20,000 to revamp, decorate and restore (a budget which she exceeded), she could not endear herself to society and the public. She was criticized for entertaining while there was a war on, but if she hadn't she would have been criticized even more severely. One of the wonderful legacies of Mary was the purchase of a seven-hundred-piece set of Bohemian cut glass; history has proven that the woman had excellent taste, but then she was from a very upper-class family despite what Washingtonians might have liked to have thought.

Mary was even criticized for holding a gala while Willie was dying. That the Lincolns did not know at the time that Willie was critically ill was never taken into consideration; it was just more ammunition for the hatemongers. The mudslingers had a field day, saying it was the judgment of God on the Lincolns that they should be punished so because of their frivolity, their dancing, entertaining and drinking. The hate letters became so awful that

Lincoln's words of wisdom spoke to the people of his day and were cherished and quoted. In that respect nothing has changed. Lincoln is still avidly quoted by reporters, politicians, writers and by people of all walks of life.

Mary instructed Stoddard to read everything first and none of the many hateful, nasty letters were to be given her. When she withdrew from most entertaining she was criticized even more for drowning herself in her grief. Considering the war, the social pressures and the tragedies she had to bear it is surprising that Mary did not have a breakdown long before Lincoln's assassination. After his death she holed herself up in her rooms, sobbing uncontrollably. Those five weeks allowed the staff of the White House to rob it of many of its treasures. Mary was not only criticized for the thefts but also because she mourned so deeply. The only ones who stood by her and helped her were her spiritualist friends. No wonder she had more respect for them than for Washington society. Mary Lincoln's ghost has never been seen in the White House. Mary was only too happy to leave the place she had been so unhappy in.

Mark Twain had this conversation with Congressman Billy Mason regarding Lincoln's legacy.

> MASON: *What a pity it was that fate did not intend that Lincoln should marry Ann Rutledge. It seems that fate governs our lives and plans history in advance.*
> TWAIN: *Yes. Had Lincoln married the dear one of his heart's love he might have led a happy but obscure life and the world would never have heard of him. Happiness seeks obscurity to enjoy itself. A good-looking milkmaid might have kept Alexander the Great from conquering the world.*
> MASON: *Well, doesn't that prove that what is to be will be?*
> TWAIN: *The only thing it proves is that what has been was.*

Why is it that Lincoln dominates the hearts and minds of Americans and non-Americans alike? No president has so influenced the thoughts of a people as did Lincoln. No president has ever been revered as he, not even Washington. Was it because Lincoln was the first to be assassinated in this country? Was it because of emancipation? Was it because he was so adamant that states did not have rights individually, as they were part of a collective United States of America and must remain one undivided, uniform entity, ruled for the common good of all its citizens? Was it because he felt that the states' rights were usurping the rights of the people and flittering them away? What was it about this tall gangly man that put an entire nation in mourning, a grief that the nation has never been able to recover from?

In 1941 Eleanor Roosevelt stated that she saw Lincoln just before the Japanese bombed Pearl Harbor. She maintained that she had an affinity with him, a rapport with the former president whom she greatly admired. Jacqueline Kennedy would sit in the Lincoln room and talk to the late president and was said to receive strength from him. She saw him shortly before they left for Dallas where President Kennedy was assassinated. How frustrating for Lincoln that he could not help only warn, not prevent or avert the tragedies that he knew were to follow. How frustrating.

President Buchanan, Lincoln's predecessor, was quite happy to leave the White House and said to Lincoln, "If you are as happy, my dear sir, on entering this house, as I am on leaving it and returning home, you are the happiest man in the country." Buchanan had running water installed in the White House, and its source was the Potomac near the Washington Canal. The river and canal were repeatedly referred to as nothing more than a sewerage outlet. Lincoln was resigned about being president but never experienced the euphoria that Buchanan thought Lincoln might feel. Lincoln had lost his first love Ann Rutledge, and Buchanan had also lost the woman he loved to illness (or perhaps suicide, the rumors stated). He never married and was the only president to have remained a bachelor his entire life. Lincoln moved into the White House on March 4, 1861.

When Willie Lincoln died of typhoid he was laid out in the White House. Lincoln kept on going down to where he lay and had the guards remove the cloth off of his precious child's face so he could look at it just one more time. He felt because Willie had died so suddenly, he couldn't accept the fact

D.W. Griffith's Abraham Lincoln starred Walter Huston. This image is from a 1940s postcard, which may have been taken from a scene in the movie. Huston played Lincoln admirably.

that he was deceased or comprehend it. Lincoln felt that the spirit Willie was always nearby and, though removed from, near his body. Is there any difference between Lincoln holding conversations with his darling Willie and James Garfield, the twentieth president, who spoke with his father all the time even though his father had succumbed to a cold he had caught while putting out a forest fire when James Garfield was only eighteen months old? Certainly Lincoln knew his son longer and more intimately than Garfield knew his father but knowing a person well, or even at all, is not a criterion for spirits to make contact. For some reason, the White House and its occupants are magnets for paranormal happenings.

Garfield only occupied the White House for four months before Charles J. Guiteau shot him. Guiteau was disgruntled that he had not received the office he desired. His shot did not go very deep and if the doctors had been more knowledgeable and had left it alone Garfield probably would have recovered. However, the doctors didn't leave the bullet alone and Garfield died from infection. Sanitary precautions were almost non-existent, at the time. Seventy-nine days after Guiteau shot Garfield, he breathed his last mortal breath. Garfield was the second president to perish from a bullet wound. Assassination history, unfortunately, would repeat itself every four terms.

The day before Garfield was assassinated he spoke with Robert Todd Lincoln in the White House. Garfield had a premonition of his own assassination and thought he could obtain an insight by speaking to Lincoln's one surviving son. McKinley was warned not to go to Buffalo.

Meeting of President LINCOLN
and Gen'l GRANT.

Lincoln had complete faith in Grant, and though the two men were very different in their habits, Lincoln was more than happy to indulge and aid Grant as he felt that Grant was the man to win the war.

The Myth and Mystery of Lincoln's Ghost

President Ulysses Grant, the hard-drinking, card-playing, cigar-smoking general who secured his place in history by defeating Lee and hence the Confederacy and preserving the Union, was a great believer in the supernatural as were his family and many of his staff. A member of his household communicated with young Willie Lincoln's spirit.

President Lyndon B. Johnson's daughter Lynda's bedroom was once Willie Lincoln's bedroom and she was very aware of Willie. Even Lady Bird Johnson had a spectral visit one evening from a cold presence who made her aware of the history and importance of her residence. Sometimes we need someone to make us aware of our surroundings and the significance of the items that make up the whole of the décor. It is a case of seeing the individual trees in the forest.

The incidents, even minor ones, are so numerous and yet so many would refute them and those who experienced them. Denying something, refusing to believe something, does not make something not so. One cannot refute all these sightings or those who perceived them. The question really is, Why? Why so many, and is there hope of rest for these restless spirits? Is there an importance for the nation in president Lincoln's continued presence? Does he in some manner act as a guardian?

Abraham Lincoln Walks at Midnight

It is portentous, and a thing of state
That here at midnight, in our little town
A mourning figure walks, and will not rest,
Near the old court-house pacing up and down,

Or by his homestead, or in shadowed yards
He lingers where his children used to play,
Or through the market, or the well-worn stones
He stalks until the dawn-stars burn away.

A bronzed, lank man! His suit of ancient black,
A famous high-top hat and plain worn shawl
Make him the quaint great figure that men love,
The prairie-lawyer, master of us all.

He cannot sleep upon his hillside now.
He is among us—as in times before!
And we who toss and lie awake for long,
Breathe deep, and start, to see him pass the door.

Portraits of Lincoln always show a careworn thoughtful person. It is the eyes one is drawn to, and the haunted look of a man who knew his doom.

The Myth and Mystery of Lincoln's Ghost

His head is bowed. He thinks of men and kings.
Yea, when the sick world cries, how can he sleep?
Too many peasants fight, they know not why;
Too many homesteads in black terror weep.

The sins of all the war-lords burn his heart.
He sees the dreadnoughts scouring every main.
He carries on his shawl-draped shoulders now
The bitterness, the folly and pain.

He cannot rest until a spirit-dawn
Shall come—the shining hope of Europe free:
A league of sober folk, the worker's earth,
Bringing long peace to Cornland, Alp and Sea.

It breaks the heart that kings must murder still,
That all his hours of travail here for men
Seem yet in vain. And who will bring white peace
That he may sleep upon his hill again?

Vachel Lindsay (1879–1931)

FORD'S THEATER AND JOHN WILKES BOOTH

There is no doubt that Ford's Theater is the most famous (or infamous) theater in America. Today it is a museum, a restored theater that once again welcomes the theater-loving public. Its claim to fame, of course, is that it is the place where for the first time a president of the United States was assassinated. The building sits on the site of the old First Baptist Church. When John Ford purchased the church he also purchased the adjoining property. As a successful theater owner in other major cities, Ford felt that a theater would be a very profitable establishment in Washington, and so it was for a time. The fact that the other building was a saloon made it a very profitable enterprise. Ford's son Harry lived above the saloon and managed the theater. Ford had created a rather compact center for entertainment, as well as a cost-effective one.

After Lincoln's assassination, the theater closed. In July of 1865 Ford tried to reopen the theater but the cry of outrage was so great that the government would not allow them to open, as the authorities were justifiably frightened of mob violence. There had been a definite reason that Lincoln had been reelected with a landslide. People truly loved him because of his honesty, which was rare in a politician, but even more so, because he had preserved the nation.

In an era of flowery speeches, Lincoln spoke to everyone as an equal, as fellow Americans and never tried to bamboozle or mislead them. He was direct, thoughtful, kind and cared more about the nation and the individuals that composed it than he did about his pocketbook.

With the Gettysburg Address he had already begun the healing and reunification of the country, which was his ultimate goal. It is not

Scene of LINCOLNS ASSASSINATION at Ford's Theater in Miniature

The photographs taken by Matthew Brady were used to restore Ford's Theater, which is once again a theater. It is also open as a museum. Old postcards and photographs are eagerly sought by social historians and researchers, as they offer such excellent documentation.

surprising, then, that as a martyr he would hold the nation's undying love, respect and affection. The country was still in mourning and the reopening of Ford's Theater would seem more than disrespectful. Also, any excuse for the puritanical element to condemn the theater or any entertainment was a perfect chance to condemn theatergoers, dancers and all entertainment as tools of the devil and cause for damnation. Just because Mary Lincoln was no longer first lady didn't mean the puritanical right wing that made her life a misery were not verbose and active. They felt that if America had problems it was because they deserved them because they did not follow such guidelines. If Lincoln was shot it was because he was a terrible drunk! The fact is Lincoln didn't particularly like the taste of liquor and what little he did drink he added sugar to. It wasn't that he was against alcohol; he just didn't have a taste for it. He once said that if it would make all his generals as good as the hard-drinking Grant he would send cases of whiskey to them. To place the blame on the victim, President Lincoln, for being shot was sinking to the lowest level imaginable. It was the, "If I don't like chocolate or think it moral to eat it, no one should be allowed it, and it should not be allowed to exist and those who eat chocolate shall be damned for all eternity" syndrome.

Ford's Theater didn't have a chance. Being a practical man of business, Ford knew the terrible reputation the building had thrust upon it by John Wilkes Booth's dastardly deed. Under pressure, Ford sold the building to the government. Ford's son who had managed the theater actually went to jail because of the Lincoln assassination, though he did not have anything to do with it. He had been friendly with John Wilkes Booth; and why should he not have been? How was he to know what Booth was going to do?

Ford's Theater became the Bureau of Records and Pension and the Army Medical Museum. In 1887 the War Department moved out and in 1893 the museum followed, as the interior of the building collapsed. The building at 511 Tenth Street NW was in ruins and twenty-two people had lost their lives while sixty-eight others were injured in the collapse. Was the building jinxed?

It may be a coincidence, but the day the building collapsed was the day Edwin Booth, a greater actor than his brother and totally

Lincoln spent considerable time traveling, whether on the campaign trail or visiting his generals and soldiers on the battlefields. It is amazing that he was not killed or kidnapped before John Wilkes Booth finally succeeded in his scheme.

68

innocent of any connection to the assassination, was buried. So many coincidences relating to Lincoln, many only peripheral, seem to be spun up into an interconnected spider web.

In 1968 the newly restored Ford's Theater was opened to the public again by the National Parks Service. In 1990 the basement museum, which was basically the par excellence collection of O.H. Oldroyd, was moved to the theater from the Petersen House.

Again, coincidence—the room that Lincoln had been taken to and died in had been rented by John Wilkes Booth a short time before. Dr. Charles Leale, a twenty-three-year-old assistant surgeon with the United States volunteers, was at the theater and, seeing the condition Lincoln was in and knowing how much traffic there was out in the streets because of the celebrating soldiers, suggested Lincoln be moved to the Petersen House, as he did not feel that the president could survive the trip back to the White House.

Also, the detective on duty when the assassination occurred, John Forrest Parker, a known alcoholic, was not where he was supposed to be but was down in the saloon having a drink. This was probably at the same time John Wilkes Booth was having his last drink before he headed into the theater where Lincoln had just received a standing ovation and Laura and Ford Keene, both friends of Booth, were performing. Was there a reason Parker was the detective that evening and was not in his place? Mrs. Lincoln had recommended him and there is strong sentiment that Secretary of War Stanton had persuaded her to have the president hire him. Mary Lincoln was always involving herself in political matters and Stanton was an extremely insistent personage. Mary was probably manipulated by Stanton and thought he was doing it because he had the president's best interests at heart.

Photographs are such an important part of social history. The documentation and the restoration of the theater are so exact because the restorers were able to use photographs taken by Matthew Brady for reference. Brady was a photographer and had spent much of his time during the Civil War photographing people like Lincoln and Booth and the soldiers on and off the battlefield. His work appeared in many papers and periodicals of the era, including *Harper's Weekly*. Brady did much to memorialize Lincoln's image during his lifetime. So too did artist caricaturist Thomas Nast, who many only remember because of his rendition of Santa Claus. Lincoln felt Nast did more to recruit soldiers for the Union than anyone else. Where most people were terrified of his caricatures and of being caught by his pen, Lincoln was delighted. Nast lionized Lincoln and did much to solidify his image with the public. Nast knew how feared he was and how much his pen empowered him. He also was convinced that what Lincoln was doing was the right thing. Not so John Wilkes Booth, a Confederate sympathizer who ran blockades and smuggled quinine to the South. Some think he was a spy and he might have been running weapons as well. When invited to the White House, Booth did not even give the president and Mrs. Lincoln the courtesy of replying to the invite. Lincoln had extended the invitation as an admirer of both the actor and his profession. He was an avid theatergoer and had seen many of the Booth clan on the stage over the years.

If Lincoln is the nucleus of the spider web it is Booth that is the spider—the mover, the maker and ensnarer, the man who made $20,000 per year as one of the top-paid actors in the country. Booth put America in mourning and ruined the lives and caused the deaths of countless people.

Booth was a man who was no stranger to death or killing. In his youth, Booth, a detester of cats, killed all the cats on the family farm in one of his fits of rage. His compassion and respect for life were extremely suspect. Supposedly, Booth's last words as he lay dying were, "Sic simper tyrannus" ("Thus always to tyrants," which happens to be the state motto of Virginia). This seems unlikely, as this is also what Booth was supposed to have shouted as he leapt from the presidential box onto the stage while escaping after the assassination. Booth was an educated, articulate man and not one to repeat when he could have used a better quote, and as a Shakespearian actor he knew many. Furthermore, he had a bullet wound in his head and was incapable of speech. This theatrical incident is just one of the many stories that may have been fabricated by sympathizers or those involved in the cover-up of his escape.

The ghostly plot thickens, with too many grays and not enough definition and evidence. Booth was at odds with his entire family in regard to the war and there was a capital rift between them. Unfortunately, "guilt by association," or in this case by relationship, ruled the day, and they too were dragged into the incident as scapegoats. There can never be enough scapegoats and if they are innocent…well, so be it; that is what scapegoats are for.

John's brother Joseph was arrested but later released. He was a Wells Fargo messenger in the Telegraph Hill area of San Francisco, which is one of the places Booth was said to harbor before he escaped to Europe. It is confusing, but then it all depends on whether you believe the person killed really was Wilkes Booth. Booth's sister Asia's husband,

Edwin Booth, the older brother of John Wilkes Booth, escaped consequences and embroilment in the witch-hunt aftermath of the assassination. He was a greater actor than his brother.

John Sleeper Clarke, and her brother Junius Booth did not fare as well. They were charged with complicity and served jail sentences in the Old Capitol Prison.

John Wilkes Booth came from the first family of the theater in America. His father was considered the greatest Shakespearian actor ever to walk across a stage in America. John, though he adored his father, resented him because of his alcoholism. The fact that he was not the actor his father was rankled him, and everyone made sure he was aware of how great his father was. People were not mean about it; they just enjoyed genuflecting on the greatness of the father. It was like comparing carnival glass to Tiffany. Both have iridescence but they are not in the same league. If Booth was jealous of his father, his relationship to his brother Edwin Booth was shaky at best. Sibling rivalry, especially when one is vying for the top spot in the pecking order, can be very unnerving and definitely unrewarding. It certainly does not make for close relationships.

The fact that they were on opposite sides of the war in their sympathies made matters even worse. Both brothers disapproved of each other, but for different reasons. Edwin was by all accounts not as handsome as his brother but was much the greater actor. Like his father, he had

This is the bed where Abraham Lincoln took his last breath. The turned-spool bed and other accoutrements of the period give one a feel of the era. Antiques, photographs, postcards and ephemera are incredible reference material for social historians.

a drinking problem, but not quite of the same magnitude, though he too missed performances because he was incapacitated from drink. Those who saw both Edwin and his father perform said the son was as great as the father, which did not sit well with John Wilkes. Because of his fame and stature and his known Union sympathies Edwin was not arrested. One's involvement in the crime did not have a rational or just effect on the how and why of one being dragged into the hysteria and guilt by association that madly reigned over the capital.

A Psalm of Life

Life is real! Life is earnest!
And the grave is not its goal;
Dust thou art and to dust thou returnest,
Was not spoken of the soul.

Henry Wadsworth Longfellow
(Lincoln's favorite poem)

The Petersen House, where Lincoln suffered his last hours, is today a pleasant building done up in antiques and furniture of the era and reproductions of a high quality. Everything is as it should be to make the restless spirits of the Lincoln era feel at home. Lincoln, for obvious reasons, is drawn to the building he spent his last living moments in.

Petersen was a German tailor who arrived in America in 1842 with only a profession to work in his favor. Only in his twenties, he opened a small tailor shop where he made a good living. In 1849 he married a German woman and built the house. Because of its proximity to the theater, thespians found it a particularly attractive place to stay. However, the boarders were also soldiers and government employees, as they too were close enough to walk to work and for some the proximity of the saloon and entertainment was a definite enticement to lodge there.

The probability is that Booth had actually slept on the same bed that the president died in. As with Ford's Theater, after the assassination things went from great to horrible. The theater was closed so no thespians boarded at the Petersen House. Frankly, many didn't want to stay in a building where their beloved president had perished. A year later the fifty-one-year-old Petersen, who had lost his health and was heavily in debt, died only to be followed by his wife the following year. In October 1871 the contents of this once busy establishment were

Across the street from Ford's Theater, President Lincoln was moved into a room and a bed where John Wilkes Booth, the president's assassin, had stayed and slept just a short time before. Irony? Coincidence? Was there more than one conspiracy surrounding the death of Lincoln?

sold to cover some of the debts, and the bed that Booth slept in and Lincoln died in was sold for eighty dollars. Some say the ghost that walks this building is Petersen, others that it is both Petersen and his wife, while still others say it is Mr. Lincoln. As Lincoln's ghost is usually seen rather than heard making noises, one can only doubt.

THE MARY SURRATT HOUSE

During the Civil War the Mary Surratt house was 541 H Street NW; it has since been renumbered 604. Mary Surratt and her family were tragically caught up in the events surrounding President Lincoln's assassination. To John Wilkes Booth, the Surratts seemed expendable, and therefore he sacrificed them to his cause. Mary's son John easily fell under the dashing actor's spell and became a conspirator with him in his plot to kidnap the president. If they could capture Lincoln they could use him as a hostage, a human ransom, to obtain the release of Confederate prisoners. John Surratt thought this a wonderful idea. Before they could put the plan into effect Lee surrendered to Grant and the terrible Civil War, which had pitted brother against brother, was over. Considering that the original plan was simply to free boys in gray it seems strange that Booth should shift his goal to that of killing the president. The war had just ended and the Confederate soldiers were already pardoned and marching on home. Lincoln was doing everything in his power to allow the soldiers to go home and resume their lives as best they could. His plans for healing the country were his first priority and were succinct. The Gettysburg Address said it all.

John Surratt was horrified by Booth's change in plans, as were many other kidnap conspirators who refused to go along with Booth's plans to kill the president. They felt there was no need and that they had lost the opportunity to do anything when Grant took Richmond. The war was over and they were ready to focus on making a new life for themselves.

Perhaps, as Booth lived in a world of theatrical fantasy, killing the president seemed a great plot for a play. The idea of bringing such a plan to fruition and into the realm of reality was horrific. Crossing from fantasy into reality should not have even been a consideration. Could Booth have had any thought for the consequences of his actions? Did he take into consideration the lives of anyone but himself? Did he see this as just another play where he was the hero, thinking that when the play was over the lights would dim and then, to thunderous applause, he and the rest of the cast (including the murdered president) would step in front of the curtain, the spotlight would shine upon them and they would take their bows? The play would have ended; then they would all go home. Was he a hero in a play in his own mind, which he could not separate from reality, or was he such a rabid fanatic that anyone could be sacrificed to his ego and vision? Or could there have been other factors, other conspiracies, hatching at the same time? Was Booth taking his orders from someone else? Someone higher up in the conspiracy that played him as a pawn as Booth himself played others?

John Surratt escaped to Canada, then to Europe and joined the Vatican Zouaves. In 1867 he was captured in Egypt, was brought back to the states and stood trial. He was acquitted. What must have been his horror to know the fate his mother suffered? How could he resign himself to the plight and sorrow of his sister Anna? Mary Lincoln did not attend the trial, however both of the Lincoln sons did and testified.

Mary Surratt's daughter Anna had been charmed beyond casualness by the handsome thespian. She had no knowledge of what Booth was about. He escorted her to the theater a few times and treated her like a great lady, but then he also escorted Bessie Hale, to whom he was purportedly engaged and who was the daughter of Senator John Parker Hale of New Hampshire. Booth was a charming character who most men liked and women were totally charmed by. He was reportedly a Don Juan, a ladies' man who women, even married ones, swooned over and succumbed to. Urban legend says that John Wilkes Booth had seduced both mother and daughter, but this is most probably not true.

One can only imagine the fear and horror Anna must have felt when, at midnight on the night Lincoln was shot, the sound of horses and shouting men was at the door. Police and the military rousted her mother from bed, pulling and shoving her, not allowing her to change her night clothing, and charged her with being a conspirator in the assassination of the president. Mary probably had no idea at the time that Booth had planned on doing such a thing. She certainly had no reason to think she would be implicated in an assassination conspiracy, or else she would not have retired to bed that evening. Her cries of protest were probably heart rendering, and young Anna saw and heard what they were accusing her mother of and her mother's horrified reaction. Fear must have enveloped both mother and daughter as well as disbelief at what had happened and what was happening. Pulled out of sleep in the middle of the night, they must have been slightly slow to realize that this was not a terrible nightmare but reality, which can be many times worse than night tremors. If Booth was such a hero, how could he condemn these innocent women to what was to be their fate? The concept of "the end justifies the means" is not a sword utilized by the just or those who feel their actions and cause are just.

In 1835, when seventeen-year-old Mary Jenkins married John Surratt she was a devout Catholic who had been educated in Alexandria by the Sisters of Charity. They went to live on a twelve-hundred-acre farm in a sparsely populated section of southern Maryland that became known as Surrattsville for about a dozen years. As more people moved into the area Mary and John turned part of their home into a store and tavern. After John died, Mary decided to take the two children and go live in Washington. She rented the place to a former Washington policeman and purchased what was to become known as the Surratt House. It was in close proximity to the centers of activity in Washington, yet just enough removed to give it tranquility and privacy. It was the perfect place for John Wilkes Booth to plot a deed that would ruin the lives of many, including Mary Surratt and her family.

Some people embroil themselves in situations that ruin their lives and bring them suffering and woes. Mary Surratt, a plain but not uncomely woman, only wanted to forget the loss of her husband and comfortably bring up her two children. Running a boardinghouse was not easy work, but then she had been used to living on a farm, running a store and living away from areas of convenience. She was used to working long hours doing hard work to make her living. She must have felt flattered and charmed at the patronage of the youthful and flamboyant thespian. Life for a widow woman was very difficult and probably rather lonely.

After the assassination of President Lincoln, Mary was arrested and tried for conspiracy of murder. Mary Surratt's trial ended on June 30, 1865. Presiding Judge Advocate General Joseph Holt was a dour man who was described as vindictive and ill mannered. He seemed to be disliked even amongst his peers but he did give the public what they wanted, which was another body upon the gallows. He resided in the Thomas Law house at First and C Streets SW, which Law built for his wife, who was the granddaughter of Martha Washington. Holt had every right to become overwhelmed with remorse, as he had denied Mary Surratt the ability and the opportunity to defend herself properly. Shortly after his decision he became a recluse and shut himself up in the Law house. It was said that Holt sat and read and reread the papers. He was obsessed with them and he became steeped in gloom and depression to the point that he boarded up the windows and lived in twilight for the rest of his days. The yard became overgrown, the house became dilapidated and in the semi-darkness he pined and ruminated. It was almost impossible to make the place a happy home after that and future residents were disturbed by the relentless pacing of Holt's ghost. The building was finally torn down so that the ghost was reduced to pacing up and down the street. It was said that Holt repressed evidence and knowingly allowed false evidence to be admitted in Mary Surratt's trial. It seems he, at least, may have received his just deserts.

If there was little or no justice or fair play in the trials, the lack of humanity to the prisoners was worse than barbaric. Besides an iron ball strapped to their legs, their heads were encased in heavy canvas padded an inch thick with cotton. They could not see or hear and there was only one tiny hole so they could be fed but could not speak. The covering was tied tightly around the neck and they could barely breathe or move. Their pain and suffering must have been great, but the injustice of perverting the Constitution by not allowing them due process via a fair trial gives credence to the government conspiracy theory. The physical restraint was tantamount to torture and the lack of hygiene must have been horrendous.

Mary Surratt was hanged on the gallows on July 7, 1865, along with George Atzerodt, Davis Herold and Lewis Powell. Mary alone of the four did not have a seventy-five-pound iron ball attached to her leg. Bound and weak, she still could not climb the gallows by herself and had to be assisted. One guard was kind enough to hold a parasol over her head to keep off the sun.

Three hundred people attended the hanging as if it were a festive occasion, including General George Custer and his new wife. This was just the type of capital entertainment that Custer would treat his wife to on her honeymoon.

It is a testimony to the human spirit and the courage of the first woman to be hanged in the United States that even after what she had physically endured, as well as the false accusations hurled at her during the trial, Mary Surratt was still conscious and courageous enough to plead for her life. Her terror and emotional turmoil must have been overwhelming. It should be noted that other women were hanged before Mary Surratt, but not since the Revolutionary War. The Salem witches were hanged, as were other women, for everything from suspected witchcraft to murder, but not since Americans had gained their independence.

Mary was unceremoniously buried in the prison yard near the scaffold she was hanged from. Pastor Jacob Walter of Saint Patrick's Church was a beneficent man who stood up for what he believed. Against protests he prayed for Mary Surratt and stood beside her at the gallows. He was the one person who showed her mercy, pity and compassion. Unfortunately he still had to watch the death of an innocent woman and live with the knowledge that he could do nothing more for her. Perhaps he was the one hero in this entire saga. He had to brave the anger and ire of even his own parishioners. Washington was full of angry people who wanted blood to be shed and they didn't care whose it was as long as they could witness it or read about it, and the news media made the most of it.

After her mother's execution, Anna put the house on the market for $4,600, which was only half of its value, but the house had such an infamous reputation that few were interested in purchasing it. Booth had ruined Mary Surratt's life and, perhaps, her repose in the hereafter. Anna had tried to have her mother released from prison and failed. She had tried to get clothing to her mother so she could be properly attired and failed. The *Evening Star* stated that Mary was never even given a change of clothing and went to her death in the same clothing she had been wearing at the moment of her arrest. Anna even tried to force her way into the White House to see President Johnson in hopes that he would reprieve Mary, but she was turned away. She had failed in every effort. How sad. How tragic. Anna gave her all and was not able to accomplish one single thing to alleviate the pain and suffering of her mother, whom she knew to be innocent. Is it not surprising, then, that after her earthly demise Anna would still go knocking at the White House door trying to gain admittance to see the president or to return to the boardinghouse she had lived in?

The Surratt boardinghouse changed hands over and over with great rapidity. The occupants continually complained of mumblings and whisperings, moanings and muffled sobs, ominous noises and creaking boards. Did the conspirators' ghosts return? Had Anna or Mary returned to their last residence? Anna's ghost has been seen at the White House banging on the door, trying to get in to see the president. All her hopes for a future were dashed and her mother had been ripped from her in such a violent way that it is not surprising that she remains earthbound until she can find a way to help her mother.

There is quite a bit of evidence that points to the fact that Booth was not actually killed when he was supposedly caught; that a red-haired person was shot in his place and was the body assumed to be Booth's. Is the Booth cover-up why Mary and the other supposed conspirators were so callously treated? Why, regardless of the crime (as the punishment if found guilty would remain the same), were they treated in such a manner? Was it to stop them from telling the truth and revealing the real conspiracy, which was to allow Booth to escape by substituting someone else in his place? How many people needed to be sacrificed in order to save one assassin? Why was it so important to save Booth? Booth was unscrupulous in his desire for self-preservation. But what of the conspirators within the government who were really behind Booth? Does Lincoln's ghost need to have justice? Like a maze the twists and turns are numerous and it is impossible to know which way to turn. Is there a way out of the maze or is it self-perpetuating and self containing?

What a Tangled Web...

I s it possible that all of these events and tragedies are interconnected? Are they all part of a grand conspiracy to make one man president? How far will some men go, to what extremes, and what price are they willing to pay in order that they obtain power? If there were such a secret organization known as The Knights of the Golden Circle and if Secretary of War Stanton was the prime mover of that organization and if he was able to eliminate the president, the vice president and the secretary of state in one evening, that would make Edwin Stanton president. Stanton could never become president by running for the office and being elected to it. The old saying is that power corrupts, but the powerful are often already corrupt and use that corruption to obtain more power.

Lincoln died and Seward survived his stabbing, while Vice President Johnson was to be murdered by George Atzerodt. Thankfully after stalking the vice president for a time Atzerodt lost his nerve and did not go through with the deed. Atzerodt was one of the four, along with Mary Surratt, who were hanged from the gibbet.

Stanton had been an attorney general in the Buchanan administration and was a holdover from the Lincoln administration into that of Johnson. Johnson was a totally self-educated man. He had never been to school and did not learn to read until after he was married. His wife taught him to read, and he made up for lost time reading and bettering himself. This was a man who had come from abject poverty and had picked himself up out of illiteracy to semi affluence and respectability. He had been chosen as vice president to replace Hannibal Hamlin because the party ticket needed to be balanced with a pro-unionist Southern Democrat. At the moment Lincoln was shot Johnson was sick in bed with typhoid fever at his home. He was awoken and rushed to Lincoln's bedside. Medically, for the safety of both men, this should never have been allowed but they were not aware of such matters as germ spreading at that time. Lincoln lay bleeding to death and Johnson, dragged to the scene suffering all the problems of typhoid, which was a very common killer, saw rooms full of spectators, including Stanton who was probably counting his chickens and taking the oath of office in his own maniacal mind as the next in line. Seeing Johnson must have been a bitter disappointment.

Johnson wanted to continue on with a lenient Reconstruction. Technically, he felt the Confederacy never left the Union because the United States was Constitutionally indissolvable. His Cabinet and Washington politicians, many of whom were radical Republicans, were of two separate minds on how the South should be treated and Johnson was never able to obtain the upper hand. He tried to implement many of Lincoln's ideas and felt Jefferson Davis and Lee, as well as the rest of the misguided Confederacy, should be treated with tolerance, respect and leniency. There was no reason to take out vengeance on a defeated foe, especially as they were fellow Americans. It could only be counterproductive and hurt the country.

Stanton was in full sympathy with the harsh Reconstruction, radical Republicans in Congress. In February of 1868 Johnson had had it up to his ears with Stanton and fired him. Stanton absolutely refused to quit his office, claiming it was his right under the Tenure of Office Act, which had just been made into law. Barricading himself in his office at the War Department, Stanton refused to leave. He finally resigned later in the year, but only after making life for those who desired a smooth transition for reunification a seemingly insurmountable nightmare.

During the time Stanton was in office he opposed the enfranchisement of blacks, women's suffrage and in general was a major cause of all the anti-black laws that were enacted in the South. Stanton was adamant that the conspirators in the Lincoln assassination be brought to trial immediately and with a brutal disregard for due process. Stanton's friend James Speed was attorney general and it was he who ruled that the conspirators would be tried in a military court. This ruling meant that Mary Surratt didn't have a chance.

During his one term of office Johnson used his veto twenty-nine times and fifteen times it was overridden. To thwart the radical Republicans was an almost impossible task, as their stand on Reconstruction was so adamant, so written in stone that they could not and would not work for the good of the nation. Reasoning with them was an impossibility and it only frustrated Johnson and made him feel ineffectual and helpless. However,

Jefferson Davis was the president of the Confederacy and, along with Lee, was the person Lincoln spent most of his wartime years trying to second guess.

Robert E. Lee was the commander of the Confederate army. Lincoln admired him as a general and a soldier.

he was courageous enough to fight them even with the odds against him. Congress desperately wanted to impeach Johnson and if it had not been for seven Republican senators who risked all to oppose the radicals, Stanton and his radical group would have won the day. Stanton was the ringleader. Maneuver and manipulate as much as he would, he would never become president, or lead the country in the direction he wanted to but he did do considerable damage. If Stanton had become president our country would probably not have survived.

In 1853 Johnson said, "There are some who lack the confidence in the integrity and capacity of the people to govern themselves. To all who entertain such fears I will most respectfully say that I entertain none…if man is not capable. And is not to be trusted with the government of himself, is he to be trusted with the government of others…Who, then, will govern? The answer must be, Man for we have no angels in the shape of men, as yet, who are willing to take charge of our political affairs." Was he speaking of Stanton, who desperately tried to usurp power and wanted to manipulate and use the government "of the people and by the people" for his own purposes?

Johnson was not a compromising deep thinker like Lincoln, but he did his best to lead the country in a more moderate direction even if he had very little regard for the educated or the elite. His opinion was that it was the middle classes, the landowning hard-working people, who counted, not the rich or the poor. The rich didn't need help, they took very good care of themselves and the poor would be taken care of and drawn into the middle classes out of necessity and the help of the middle class itself. With Stanton in the Cabinet Johnson was unable to implement many of the laws and programs he felt were important. He fought a valiant battle against Stanton and his cronies.

In the book *The Reincarnation of John Wilkes Booth*, Dr. Dell Leonardi regressed, through hypnotism, a young man, who said in a previous life he was John Wilkes Booth. The fact that intensive research vindicated much of what he said is extremely seductive for those who feel there were multiple conspiracies going on at the time of the Lincoln assassination and that Stanton was in the thick of it. The web is so interwoven and the maze so complicated it is impossible not to become entangled or lost. There are just too many pieces of the puzzle missing with the reason for their being missing extremely suspect. However, whether what we know or are allowed to know is truth or terminological inexactitudes, it certainly is beyond the perimeters of melodrama!

LAFAYETTE SQUARE

O nce known as President's Square, it was later renamed to honor
Lafayette, but is often referred to as tragedy square. Directly across
from the White House, it was the logical site for many of the early homes
and buildings to be erected. Today few of the original buildings remain. So
many murders have occurred here and so many unexplained happenings,
mysteries and eerie occurrences have taken place here, many of which are
interconnected, that the magnet theory applies. Why so many tragic deaths?
Many feel the magnetism and attraction the spiritual world has for this area
is because it is a highly polarized spot.

Washington has grown and changed more than most cities over the years.
During the Lincoln administration, the secretary of state was William H.
Seward, who worked in the building next to the White House. We may
thank him for the purchase of Alaska from the Russians but at the time,
this visionary was ridiculed. Seward was also instrumental in the annexing
of the Midway Islands. He was an expansionist and if he had been given
his way America would be twice its size today. Seward purchased what had
once been the Washington Club in the early 1860s. He and his family were
quite aware of the haunting of the house by Philip Barton Key.

Key had been murdered by Daniel Sickles, a sometimes congressman from
New York. Sickles had married the seventeen-year-old Teresa because he felt
she would be an asset to his career. This worked out quite well for about five
years and then Teresa fell in love with and had an affair with Philip Barton
Key, the son of the amateur poet who wrote our national anthem.

Washington being Washington, a city plagued by intrigue and gossip,
someone was kind enough to give Sickles a note telling him when and where

his wife would be meeting her paramour. He confronted her, she begged for her life and he spared it after having her sign a letter in front of two witnesses that she had committed adultery. Two days later, Sickles accosted Key and killed him. The jealous husband—perhaps more likely ego-bruised—had the perfect alibi to remove someone from the scene he did not particularly care for. Teresa died a few years later and she is supposed to haunt the house while Key may be seen waving his white handkerchief from the street below, which was their signal.

Sickles was quite a strange character and had donated his leg, which he lost at the battle of Gettysburg, to the Army's National Medical Museum. During his lifetime he would regularly go and visit it. Even after his death he continued to visit his leg. Perhaps it was habit, but the man had an incredible ego and he probably just enjoyed the notoriety of being on a first-name basis with an item in a museum!

Sickles often dined at the White House and Mary Lincoln had thought him a kind and nice man. To others he was delightful and charming but that is not the criteria that make a good husband and marriage.

The house William Seward moved into, a house with a reputation for being haunted by Teresa Sickles on the inside and Key on the outside, may have been what saved William Seward's life. Louis Powell, aka Paine, was the son of a Baptist minister, a deserter from the Confederate army and was assigned the task of killing Seward, who happened to be in bed at the time with an injured leg resulting from a severe fall from his carriage. Because someone or something made so much noise, Seward's son and servant woke up and went to Seward's rescue. One could say that the racket was caused by Powell but others are more inclined to think that Philip Barton Key was the source that sounded the warning—the dead alerting the living and warning them that danger was present. Unfortunately, Seward's wife, who was an invalid, took a turn for the worse because of the incident and passed away a few months later while his young daughter, who was unfortunate enough to witness the event, went into shock and died within a year. Seward did recover from the attack but he had lost heart and, though he served under President Johnson, he did not feel capable of executing his post in a manner he felt it deserved. In 1869 Seward retired to his hometown of Auburn, New York, and within three years he too passed on.

The house changed hands quite a few times and then was purchased by the YWCA in the 1880s. The banging and noises were even too much for them and in 1895 the building was demolished.

There is a slight problem, however, regarding the haunting by Philip Barton Key. Key always was seen *outside* the house. Why, on the night of the attempted assassination, did he decide to mosey on in? Some said the noises heard after Seward passed away were Seward himself and that he was attempting to be reunited with his wife and daughter, whom he was sure had died as a direct result of the assassination attempt. Perhaps he felt guilty, as he was the target and he was the one who survived. But why blame the house and those who moved in after he had sold it and moved out?

There is more to this mystery that only breeds questions not answers. After the house was demolished Seward, or whoever the noisemaker was, ceased the din, which seems reasonable enough, as one cannot haunt a house that isn't there. It may have been a case of a poltergeist activated by the daughter, due to immense stress, on that evening. One will never know.

Lafayette Square has had more than its share of psychic problems. Major Rathbone and his wife had lived there and even after he resigned from the military and accepted a post he continued to be haunted by the Lincoln assassination. He had been severely wounded that evening as he sat in the presidential box with the president and first lady. Due to the tender nursing of his wife he did recover physically. Mentally it was a different story. Here he was courting the woman he was to marry and later murder, sitting in the box with the extremely popular president, chatting and enjoying a very pleasant comic play and in seconds his whole life was torn asunder. In his mind he probably felt he had let the nation and the president down by not saving his life and averting Booth's shot. Irrational as this might seem it is part of "survivor's guilt." Rathbone not only did not have the opportunity because of the surprise factor of John Wilkes Booth bursting into the presidential box, but he also had no way of knowing that the guard was not posted outside the door as he was supposed to be. He certainly was not privy to the fact that Booth would attempt to assassinate the president.

Rathbone's body survived his suicide attempt and he was certified as insane. Muffled sobs of a tormented man crying his heart out were heard coming from his home on Lafayette Square after his death, just as they did when he was still alive and raving in his remorse and madness.

St. John's Church, located at 1525 H Street NW, was designed by Benjamin Latrobe and has been known as the church of presidents. Every president since the church opened in June of 1816 has attended services in its hallowed halls. Also, Presidents Madison, Monroe, Jackson, Van Buren, Harrison, Taylor, Tyler, Fillmore and Buchanan were actually parishioners. Latrobe, who had rebuilt the White House after the War of 1812, was also chosen to build the church, which makes it the second oldest building on the square. Its cornerstone was laid on September 14, 1815. Latrobe cherished this creation of his above all others as he described it as having made Washingtonians who had never been so, religious. He refused payment for his work and was the first organist of the church.

Classically styled, the building is in the form of a Greek cross. In 1822 a triple-tiered steeple was erected and a one-thousand-pound bell was cast by Paul Revere's son out of a cannon that had been captured from the War of 1812.

Some of the stained-glass windows were produced in France in the 1880s by Madame Veuve Lorin. The building has been enlarged and modified but has kept its original integrity and design. President James Monroe was the first president to worship in the church and pew fifty-four has always been designated for the use of presidents and is so marked by a brass plaque.

It is said when the bell tolls for the death of an important Washingtonian, on that night at midnight six great Washingtonians file into the church and sit on the beautiful old bench that has acquired a patina from having been sat upon for almost two hundred years. There in pew fifty-four the white-robed spirits sit with their hands folded in prayer. The six pay their respects and vanish. It is an enigma that with so many portraits of the important people from the founding days of our country hanging in museums, public buildings, galleries, etc., that no one is able to identify these spirits. If they occupy the presidential pew would they not be past presidents? And which great men do they choose to honor and why? Speculating on the unknown and unexplained amuses some people, baffles others and consumes others. Curiosity is one of mankind's most endearing attributes.

THE CAPITOL

O n September 18, 1793, when George Washington laid the granite
cornerstone for the Capitol building, the construction crew consisted
of 90 slaves and there were only 820 residents in the city. The slaves that
worked on the Capitol were not farmhands but artisans who were hired out
by their owners to generate further income for their owners. It took seven
years for the first section to be completed and Congress was able to move from
Philadelphia to its new home.

However, even with seven expansions the building has never been quite what
it could have been if today's technology had been available. Badly lit, damp and
dreary corridors winding about with a plethora of rooms make the building
difficult to navigate and the basements and subbasements are infinitely worse.

Seven architects submitted designs and William Thornton, a physician,
painter and inventor, submitted the winning design. For his design he received
a plot of land to build on and five hundred dollars. Thornton was an amateur
architect but his design was impressive and stately, which was something
the Capitol needed. George Washington lauded the building as "grandeur,
simplicity and convenience."

Thornton asked permission to submit a design three months after the
competition was to have ended, and as the judges were not happy with any
of what had been submitted already they acquiesced. Thomas Jefferson
commented that the plan that was submitted "captivated the eyes and
judgment of all." Being an architect himself Jefferson was in a good position
to judge the design. To be fair to all of the contestants there were very few
trained architects in America at the time and it is amazing that so many
decent designs that were structurally sound were submitted.

This picture-perfect image masks the unhappy, the disenfranchised, the disappointed, the unfinished business that have left shades of yesterday roaming within the halls of these government buildings.

Thornton was born on the island of Tortola in the West Indies in 1739. He studied medicine in Scotland, lived in Paris for a while and then moved to America in 1787. He may not have had the architectural background that Hallet and others did but he knew what he had envisioned and was willing to fight for its correct implementation. However, many modifications were made because of the interference of would-be designers and bureaucrats.

It is said that during the War of 1812 Thornton pled with the British officer in charge to spare the building. Unfortunately it, like most of Washington, was reduced to cinders. After it was burnt the reconstruction was closer to the original design and instead of sandstone it was constructed from marble.

Stephen Hallet had been second runner-up in the contest to design the building. He was given the job of construction overseer on Thornton's draft. He was fired in 1794, as he wanted to change things by using his own designs. It was as if a much lesser painted decided to repaint the mouth of the *Mona Lisa*!

The building has 540 rooms and 16½ acres of floor space. Ghostly stories about the building began almost from the beginning. A stonemason's body was found during one of the renovations, trapped within a wall holding his trowel. It was said he had had an altercation with a carpenter who

GEORGE WASHINGTON

George Washington chose the site that was named after him. He spent much of his time turning the swamp that became Washington, D.C., into a great city. His attention to detail and powers of persuasion were responsible for the genesis of the nation's capitol.

murdered him by smashing his head in with a brick and then concealing the unfortunate mason's body in the wall using the mason's own tools. He was repeatedly seen going in and out of the wall on the Senate side of the building. In the late 1850s a workman fell from the dome of the rotunda and began repeating his free fall, reenacting his path to the rotunda every year on the day that he fell.

The ghosts of workmen are not as numerous as those of famous men who spent considerable time in the building, such as John Quincy Adams, the sixth president. Adams once described himself in his diary, "I am a man of reserved, cold, austere, and forbidding manners. My political adversaries say I am a gloomy misanthrope, and my personal enemies, an unsocial savage. With a knowledge of the actual defect I have not the pliability to reform it." He wrote to his wife about the fact that he lacked charisma and was not popular. It is interesting how he perceived himself and how others saw him. He was an incredible orator and was the most successful diplomat of his era. Regardless of what political post he held he was adamantly ethical. John Quincy Adams, like his father John Adams, the second president, was decidedly anti-slavery and did everything he could to curtail it.

Adams's dying words were "This is the end of the earth,…I am content." He was eighty years old, his career had been brilliant and he had led a particularly exciting life. As a boy of eight he and his mother Abigail watched the battle of Bunker Hill from the nearby vantage point of Penns Hill. John Quincy Adams was a multilingual intellectual who served as ambassador, secretary of state, president, state senator, U.S. senator and was a published author as well as an excellent orator. Yet he also suffered from depression and melancholia. Why is it that his ghost is often seen in Statuary Hall? Is it that he never finished his speech about the Mexican war? Does "Old Man Eloquent" need to have his say? Here was a man who, after he left the presidency, returned to Congress for nine more terms, and he was just as passionate about the Mexican war as he had been about the Revolutionary War. Here was a man who was the prime mover and negotiator for the Treaty of Ghent. Here was a man who had spent time in Europe and Russia and knew many of the heads of countries and was friends with them even before he became president. Here was a man who, until the age of seventy-nine, went skinny-dipping in the now-polluted Potomac River and swam for miles. This was the man who, every night when he went to bed said his prayer, "Now I lay me down to sleep. I pray the lord my soul to keep. If I should die before I wake. I pray the lord my soul to take." This was a man of substance and stature and yet his shadow and form are still bound to his old stamping grounds. Does he feel he still has advice to give and tasks that need to be done?

Statuary Hall is where Congress was held in the days of John Quincy Adams, but he is not the only figure that is seen there. Guards sometimes complain that the hall reverts back physically to being the old House chamber and all the members are gathered there. What is there about Statuary Hall that makes the guards so uneasy and dread nighttime among the deep shadows that are cast by the many marble statues?

Is the weight of the innumerable statues that grace this hall more than the building's foundation can handle?

The Capitol

At midnight on New Years Eve, when the clock strikes twelve, an illumination, a prosperous glow, permeates the hall and from their pedestals the shadows take form and begin a stately dance to celebrate the survival of the nation for one more year. Do the great figures of yesteryear fear that we will perish and that it is cause to celebrate yearly that we still have not flittered away the freedoms that they worked so hard for and some of them died for?

The first guard to see the statues descending from their pedestals was so shaken with fear that he quit the building. However, he is only one of many that have seen the spectral happenings of Statuary Hall and have been unnerved by them. Personally, I should think this would be the greatest place to be on New Years Eve. Some people just don't know how lucky they are! And what of the ghost of the Capitol guard who still is heard walking about the corridors late at night? Who or what is he looking for?

There has always been unease about the amount of sheer weight that the statues collectively place on the floor and whether the foundation is sound enough to maintain that amount of tonnage. However, there have also been questions about the structural soundness of the Capitol dome and it seems to be holding out quite nicely. It was predicted in the 1960s that the

Will the dome over the capitol fall during an earthquake as has been predicted? Do the statues in Statuary Hall really dance at midnight on New Year's Eve?

dome would fall in an earthquake. Actually there is a tremendous amount of controversy about the condition of the Capitol building and its many problems. It has been said that the building is sinking, the foundations are shaky and the walls are crumbling. There has been considerable work done over the years to the building but it was not always sufficient or logical.

In 1808 Benjamin Latrobe had an altercation with his construction superintendent John Lenthal. Latrobe, being the architect, would not listen to Lenthal when he insisted on a particular type of arch for support that would prevent not only stress but would also keep the building from collapsing. Latrobe thought he knew better and felt the arch would ruin the design and would be unsightly. He pulled down the support and was killed by the falling debris. His last words were a curse on the building. In 1980 architects made repairs using modern technology and removed the supports. Many think that the west front wall is doomed and Lenthal's curse will come to fruition. If an earthquake did hit the District of Columbia the dome probably would not hold.

President Garfield's ghost still haunts the Capitol corridors where his body lay in state, and the Unknown Soldier is said to appear whenever an important person is laid in state there. He marches up to the coffin, salutes and departs. What is the magnet that draws so many back to Washington and its powerhouse buildings? Is it the location and its proximity to so much water, which is a great conduit for the paranormal? Why is it that so many sightings take place when an important personage has met his demise?

There are so many sightings and so many ghosts in this area that they might just have an overpopulation problem. It is said that most of them are not aware of the existence of any others. Why are there so many sightings and so many people who are so adamant that they have seen people who are not supposed to be in our world? Or are they supposed to be and we just haven't figured it all out?

It is one thing to see George Washington, but why on his horse? Washington may have had a great rapport with his stallion and he may repeat his last ride through Washington toward Mount Vernon but why would his horse want to repeat the ride with him sufficiently enough to become a specter? Sometimes it seems almost silly but it is a haunting question. Why do animals join the ranks of the ghostly?

Why does the demon cat haunt the Capitol? The pun of referring to him as DC—demon cat, District of Columbia—is clever, but why refer to the unfortunate critter as a demon? Yes, he is known to be a portend of something terrible and his appearance does scare the guards or whoever he appears in front of, but why demonize the poor feline? It is like shooting the messenger because one does not like the message or his mode of delivering it.

U. S. Capitol

Beauty, Symbolism, Idealism and Government were portrayed to make people feel more patriotic and more accepting that the people in power were doing the right things for the country.

Unification began with Washington but did not end with Lincoln. "I am not a Virginian, I am an American" was the sentiment Washington wanted all Americans to have and believe in. He felt that only a strong central government could preserve the country and states' rights could destroy it.

Washington was the only president who did not serve his term as president in the city named after him. John Adams was the first to be president in the new capital, the District of Columbia.

Because Washington was built on swampland and because of its close proximity to water, the rat overpopulation in the District needed to be addressed quickly. To solve the problem, they followed the example of other large cities and imported cats to catch the rats. The District became overrun by well-fed cats until the rat population became so sparse that the cats also dwindled in numbers due to lack of food. Some became domesticated and some of the feral cats took jobs elsewhere, moving on to green fields and barnyards in Virginia and Maryland.

Washington never suffered from the plague, or Black Death, which was carried by the flea-carrying rats, but the city's residents found themselves with another problem, a single supernatural cat. This is not just any cat but a cat that seems immortal, as it has been around much longer than nine lives would allow. It seems this cat has supernatural powers and can increase in size from normal cat size to that of a lion! It carefully stalks its prey and then, when the chosen victim sees the seemingly harmless small black cat, it swells into mammoth proportions (but not altering its cat-like appearance) then leaps at the person. The cat's purring turns into a ferocious snarl that echoes through the corridor. Now, anyone confronted with such an animal justifiably would be frightened out of their wits. They would either scream, faint or turn and run, which is what those who have encountered this unwelcome harbinger tend to do, unless they are totally frozen with fear. Having sprung at his victim and supposedly accomplished his task, which remains unknown to us, the demon cat vanishes into thin air. It is said that one guard had a heart attack after the encounter. However, it doesn't seem that harming anyone physically is the cat's intent. His appearances coincide with national tragedies and the changing of administrations. Why a cat should care about what happens to the government or those involved in it is an unsolvable question. Why it picks on guards who have nothing to do with policy or the enactment of crimes is more than a mystery. It doesn't seem to accomplish any purpose, as being warned assumes you have a chance to avert the tragedy. That it happens on the eve of a change of administration is probably a tragedy for some but for others it is a cause for celebration. Why does this cat appear and what, if anything, does it accomplish?

How does one become earthbound and why? For instance, why would Pierre Charles L'Enfant's shadowy figure pace the corridors of the Capitol? We know Congress treated him poorly and he never was paid for the work he did but is that enough reason to bind oneself to a building? L'Enfant was a French engineer who was a friend of Lafayette and Washington. His plans for the capital city were a bit grandiose and impractical but then, who could blame him? He envisioned a Paris of his design and making but it was slightly impractical, and he did not take into account that he was dealing with a Congress whose members felt that only their opinion, and those that agreed with them, was valid. Was it L'Enfant's fault he could not distinguish a bureaucrat from a politician? So why is this sloppy little Frenchman, with his parchment tucked underneath his arm, still roaming about Congress?

THE LINCOLN MEMORIAL

O n Memorial Day, May 30, 1922, Supreme Court Chief Justice William Howard Taft dedicated the Lincoln Memorial. From the moment Lincoln died discussions and bickering began about a suitable shrine and monument to the first martyred president. In 1867, an informal Lincoln monument commission was begun. It wasn't until 1901 that the McMillan Commission decided that the monument would be placed in West Potomac Park. Why this swampy area, which was over land that had once been under the Potomac River, was chosen seemed an enigma. It also became the cause of much arguing and debate. In 1911 after all the protest had been disregarded two architects, Henry Bacon and Russell Pope, submitted the ultimate classical design of a building resembling the Parthenon on the Acropolis in Athens, which was dedicated to the goddess Athena who was the patron of that city state. The Acropolis represented civilization and culture and was where Solon the lawgiver walked, as did Socrates and Plato. It was a befitting design. The cornerstone was set in December of 1914.

Daniel Chester French was chosen to execute the statue and Jules Guerin to design two murals for either end of the building (*Emancipation* is on the north wall and *Unification* is on the south wall). A death mask made of Lincoln when he died by the sculptor Leonard Volk was used to gain an exact image of Lincoln. Daniel Chester French was one of the renowned sculptors of his day and he was extremely meticulous with his work. French made many models before he decided on the one that we see today dominating the memorial. It soon became apparent to him that the size of the statue was much too small and needed to be doubled. The cost of the marble for the statue was $61,000 including the pedestal. There

Taft was six foot two and weighed 332 pounds. His prodigious body was always being put on a diet but that didn't help him much. Not even the embarrassment of getting stuck in the bathtub could curb his appetite.

The Lincoln Memorial

Whether Secretary of War or president, Taft loved to eat in Roman proportions. The White House was a feast for Taft as the amount of state dinners and banquets were exactly what this gourmet demanded.

were twenty-eight blocks of Georgia marble used. In 1920 the workmen began assembling the twenty-eight-piece statue and it was completed in May of 1921.

One of the wonderful details of the statue was included because of French's son who was deaf. The sculptor incorporated a tribute to those who suffered from hearing loss in a subtle but endearing way. Lincoln's left hand is shaped to make the letter *A* in sign language, while the right hand forms the letter *L*.

Much has been written of Lincoln's homeliness, his gangly unattractiveness, but was he really? French used the death mask to create the likeness of Lincoln, and what we see in this incredible statue is the might and sensitivity, yes, and even a majesty and power that exuded from the man. No one looking at the statue of Lincoln, or for that matter the many depictions of him from the days even before he was president, can say a man who oozed such a spiritual aura was homely. Lincoln was probably the most spiritual president that has ever sat in the White House. It is not words but deeds that count, and in Lincoln's case they were one and the same. That might be the reason that the Lincoln Memorial, sparkling in white marble, means more to many Americans than all the other buildings in the capital. It is to the Lincoln Memorial people come to pay honor to freedom. It is to the Lincoln Memorial people come to speak to a statue that they feel personifies the essence of all that holds this country together. It is at the Lincoln Memorial

From his seat Lincoln can see the Potomac, Robert E. Lee's home and Arlington Cemetery. He was besieged in his presidency by those who tried to manipulate him but his honesty and common sense prevailed and have become legendary.

IN THIS TEMPLE
AS IN THE HEARTS OF THE PEOPLE
FOR WHOM HE SAVED THE UNION
THE MEMORY OF ABRAHAM LINCOLN
IS ENSHRINED FOREVER

Interior of Lincoln Memorial, Washington. D. C.

Lincoln's ghost is said to appear before those who stand at his statue and speak to him in sincerity and need. The statue was sculpted by Daniel Chester French, who utilized the death mask of the martyred president to make him look as he appeared in life.

No president has been as loved or hated as Lincoln was. It was painful to Mary Lincoln that members of her family were almost all fighting for the Confederacy. There is no question that her first loyalty was to her husband and the preservation of the United States. Regardless of what side one was on, his valor, sincerity and gentleness were apparent. Here was a man who was great because he did what he believed in and what had to be done, but did it with mercy, graciousness and thought.

Memorial Day was implemented to heal the wounds of the nation by honoring both sides of the Civil War. The Confederacy and the Union both lost soldiers, all of whom were Americans.

that Eleanor Roosevelt, disgusted with the Daughters of the American Revolution for refusing to allow black opera singer Marian Anderson to sing at Constitution Hall, set up, with the help of Secretary of the Interior Harold Ickes, a concert for all Americans, regardless of race, creed, ethic ancestry or political affiliation.

The Lincoln monument is a symbol of a united country, not fifty discombobulated states all doing their own thing. Lincoln was a man of the people regardless of how and when or even why they came to this country or even how rich or poor they were. He had gambled all on keeping this country from the evils of states' rights. "United we stand—Divided we fall." To him it was as simple as that. If Eleanor Roosevelt had not stood up against the injustice of the DAR, years later Dr. Martin Luther King Jr. would not have been able to stand at the memorial and, in front of twenty-five thousand freedom marchers, have given his "I Have A Dream" speech on August 28, 1963.

The Lincoln Memorial has become the symbol for emigrants, the downtrodden, the disenfranchised. This may just be the reason that so many people over the years have said they have seen Lincoln's statue smile or that they have seen or spoken to Mr. Lincoln there. How many radio broadcasts and movies have been made using the memorial as part of the story and the hero or heroine speaking to the statue or Lincoln himself? That one is awed or inspired by the beauty and gravity of the statue and the memorial is not surprising but why are so many people comforted by it and feel that the Lincoln presence illuminates the entire city?

The inscription behind Lincoln reads "In this temple, as in the hearts of the people, for whom he saved the Union, the memory of Abraham Lincoln is enshrined forever."

THE LIBRARY OF CONGRESS

John Adams authorized the creation of the Library of Congress on April 24, 1800, and its cost was $5,000. Seven hundred and forty volumes plus three maps constituted the nucleus of the library that was to be used by Congressmen so that they could research laws, rules and regulations and prepare themselves for debates and legislation. However, along came the War of 1812 and the library, which had grown to over three thousand volumes, was used to fuel the blaze that razed Washington.

After the destruction, Thomas Jefferson offered to sell, at cost, his own personal library to the nation and after much debate, in January of 1815 Congress agreed. Jefferson needed money, so his offer to sell the government the books at cost was generous. In 1825 another fire burned a selection of books (essentially duplicates) and then on Christmas Eve in 1851 a serious fire destroyed more than thirty-five thousand volumes, which included the Jefferson Library. The value of these books today would be phenomenal but in 1851 the loss was even greater, as books were treated as priceless knowledge and considered a status symbol to own. Much of our country was still illiterate and those who could read and owned books were treated with respect. Money was allocated to rebuild the library and along with the third of the books that had not been reduced to cinders, they were moved to another location, the west front of the Capitol building.

In 1864 President Lincoln appointed Ainsworth Rand Spofford as librarian of Congress. From 1864 to 1897 Spofford turned a small library into an inclusive large one. He convinced Congress to rewrite the copyright laws. After that, it was required that two copies of every book, pamphlet, map, document, etc., be submitted to the Library of Congress. This meant that no longer would the library be devoted to only those books that were pertinent to the law and government but to all subjects. It was a stroke of true genius as it cost the government nothing. In the first twenty-five years the law was in effect the library received 371,636 books, 257,153 magazines, 289,617 musical scores, 73,817 photographs, 95,249 prints and 48,048 maps. Add to that Congressional records and documents and it not only adds up to a massive collection but it also meant that there was a major housing shortage for this wealth of information.

It took two years, but in 1873 Spofford was successful in getting Congress to allocate money for a building to house the massive and constantly growing collection. John L. Smithmeyer and Paul J. Pelz submitted a design that was very Italian Renaissance in feel and was fashioned after a melding of the British Museum, the Paris Opera House and the Bibliotheque Nationale. It was an impressive design. Unfortunately, there were those who did not approve of the design and, committees being committees, wanted to enact all types of major changes. Finally the plans, though heavily modified, were accepted. In 1885 authorization for the purchase of the land took place so that building could begin in 1886.

Construction was halted for over six months because of all of the mayhem resulting from disagreements between contractors and architects. Finally on November 1, 1897, after difficult bureaucratic battles, the building was opened to the public. What had begun only for members of Congress was now the library of the nation.

By the 1930s the building was already too small for the millions of volumes that needed to be stored, so the John Adams building with its crisp art deco design was erected. In 1980 the James Madison Memorial Building opened. The main building was of course named for Thomas Jefferson who dearly loved books and reading. It is said that the three buildings are rapidly running out of space and a fourth building will be necessary in the near future. Perhaps it will be named after a mere printer, Benjamin Franklin. How that would have pleased "Poor Richard." (Benjamin Franklin wrote and printed *Poor Richard's Almanac*, which was full of pithy and sensible sayings. It has always been great reading and many people, especially politicians, quote it regularly.)

Housed in these three buildings that compose the Library of Congress is not just books and ephemera but also the social history of our country and the world. If the library of Ptolemy in Alexandria, Egypt, had not been burnt how much richer and more advanced would world civilization have become? We might have avoided the incomprehensible book burnings by religious zealots and madmen like Fra Savonarola during the rein of death and terror practiced during the inquisition. There may have not been an era known as the Dark Ages. Here we are centuries later rediscovering things that were known thousands of years before because books and knowledge were not understood and were hated and feared. The Library of Congress is one of the great wonders of our modern world. Is it any wonder that even Mr. Jefferson is occasionally seen still reading and perusing there? What a perfectly lovely place to come back to visit and keep up on current events!

There was an old miserly librarian who worked for many years in the old Library of Congress area who had a great mistrust of banks. Having the advantage of knowing which books were seldom, if ever, read he began to hide his money in those never-perused volumes. Unfortunately for the old codger, he had a heart attack one day and died without having had the opportunity to inform his family of where he had hidden the money or to have time to move it to a place his family could access it. His ghost was said to come and rummage through book after book in search of his treasure, but as the books had been moved to the Jefferson building since the time of the man's demise and were no longer on the shelves on which he had placed them he could not find the money. When these volumes were again moved to another building or section it was found that money had been hidden in some of the books. Over six thousand dollars, which in those days was a healthy sum of money, was found in various volumes. The poor old ghost is still returning to the section just west of the rotunda searching for the shelves and the books where he had hidden his money. He obviously has not found his way into the new sections and no one has bothered telling him that his treasure was found and is no longer extant. In this case it is quite evident what holds this ghost and makes him return over and over again.

WOODROW WILSON

A merica's twenty-eighth president was an enigma, probably even to himself. There are many similarities between Woodrow Wilson and Abraham Lincoln. Wilson described himself once with a little ditty:

> *For beauty I am not a star*
> *there are others more handsome by far*
> *But my face I don't mind it*
> *For I am behind it*
> *It's the people in front that I jar.*

True, Wilson was not a movie idol in looks and he wore glasses from the time he was eight years old, but he was distinguished looking. He compared himself to a dormant volcano—calm on the outside but boiling cauldron on the inside. His Irish half and his Scottish half were not compatible and his personality and nature were in constant conflict. In public he oozed the self-confidence we expect from a leading politician but he was not comfortable with strangers and was shy and almost withdrawn when with those he did not know well. Small gatherings were a great trial for him. Some say Wilson brooded, others that he was introspective. They said the same thing about Lincoln.

Wilson's first wife, Ellen Louise Axson, died on August 6, 1914, of Bright's disease. Wilson was distraught about the loss of his wife and became morose. At fifty-eight he remarried Mrs. Edith Bolling Galt, a forty-three-year-old widow. Edith was a good match for Wilson as she was strong-minded and quite prepared to work for the country. Adamant that she should be part

The tragedy of Woodrow Wilson was that what he was not able to accomplish destroyed his spirit and his health. His vision was great and for the good of human kind but the greed and avarice of others was so much greater.

of the work and observations that affected every American family during World War I, she led as an example of what could and should be done to help with the war effort. Edith had sheep grazing on the White House lawn, gasless Sundays, meatless Mondays, wheatless Tuesdays and other days of abstinence, which were strictly observed in the White House. Edith urged others to do their duty for the soldiers. After President Wilson's stroke it was her care in presenting to him only papers that were pertinent which made the White House, and hence the government, run smoothly. It was important that the nation and the world not know what physical problems the president had or to what extent.

Wilson's career was an admirable one. He was president of Princeton University (1902–10), governor of New Jersey (1911–13), and then spent eight years in the White House. During World War I and after Wilson was very aware of the need to prevent a second war, which he was certain would occur if a League of Nations was not formed.

Globalization is not something new, only the expression is. It has been around since before the Romans. With the technology of the day armies could be moved faster and so could armaments and rations. Unfortunately, it also meant people would die faster. Wilson tried desperately to avoid being drawn into a world war but after the sinking of the Cunard Liner *Lusitania* off the coast of Ireland, on May 7, 1915, taking the lives of 1,198 including that of 120 Americans, public opinion was so strong that it was only a matter of time before America had to join the allies. Germany's submarine attacks on passenger liners and sneak attacks on merchant vessels giving no warning made sure that there were not any survivors. This did not sit well with the American people. Nor did the execution of nurse Edith Cavell on October 12, 1915, by the Germans. Newspapers and magazines were full of stories of the deportations and systematic genocide of the Armenian Christians by the Turks who were Germany's ally. When Germany's foreign minister, Zimmerman's letter was intercepted to the German minister in Mexico, America had no choice but to enter the war. The release of the letter in 1917 offering financial support to Mexico and the idea that Mexico should reconquer New Mexico, Texas and Arizona infuriated the American people. Amusingly there were some who thought this might be a good idea but most Americans were outraged and were eager to fight the German monster, which seemed so eager to devour the entire world.

When the Armistice was signed on November 11, 1918, more than three hundred thousand Americans had perished, fifty-three thousand were killed in action and sixty-three thousand died from war-related diseases or accidents. The amount of wounded soldiers missing limbs that returned after the "Great War" was staggering and yet it did not prevent the next one. Wilson was positive that there would be a second war in the not so distant future if a League of Nations was not actively in place. He lobbied Congress and the Senate and ruined his health doing so. He was obsessed by the vision of another global war that would be a larger and crueler version of the one they had just fought with the Kaiser.

The fact that the United States never did join the League of Nations was a bitter disappointment to Wilson. The opposition didn't want it; they wanted to pursue their own economic agendas, which included trade with Turkey. Two of the major objectives Wilson was never able to accomplish gnawed at him, frustrated him and finally took a toll on his health which could not be mended.

So many gods, so many creeds,
So many paths that wind and wind.
While just the art of being kind
Is all the sad world needs.

Ella Wheeler Wilcox

That the nineteenth amendment passed and women finally received the right to vote was a triumph for Wilson but not, he judged, when placed beside his two failures. The failure of the League of Nations because America did not join it and his unsuccessful hope of returning to the Armenian Christians their traditional lands where they could live without being persecuted by the Turks were tragedies that he took very personally. Wilson just couldn't accept them. Unfortunately, Wilson's fears for the future came true with a vengeance. Two and a half million Armenians plus other Christians were killed by the Turks, followed by World War II and Adolph Hitler, smiling and saying, "Who now remembers the Armenians?" as he signed the papers to exterminate the Jews. Hitler had learnt, or so he thought, a valuable lesson from the Young Turks, and for a while it brought riches into his coffers and rallied the people around him giving him that which he desired above all, power.

Wilson's physical decline began in 1919 and marred the last years of his presidency and his ability to fight and obtain his objectives. He left office in 1921 and moved into a lovely brick home at 2340 S. Street Northwest, just off Embassy Row. His last words were on February 1, 1924: "I am a broken piece of machinery. When the machinery is broken...I am ready." He died on February 3, 1924. In his final years, Wilson, a collector of canes, shuffled about the house using one. He had lapses of memory, brooded continually and often broke down crying. Wilson's ghost has been heard in the house shuffling about on his cane and sobbing. Residents and guests alike have heard the president's grieving and anguished cries and moans.

The United Nations, an evolved League of Nations, is alive and well and one can easily assume this might please the former president as at least one of his major disappointments has been righted. As for Armenia, this country declared independence and is no longer a Soviet Socialist Republic state. An extremely poor country, she is fighting for survival against her oil-rich neighbors who would like to obliterate this ancient nation whose main crime is to not practice the same religion as its neighbors. Is Wilson dismayed that the first Christian nation is still being persecuted and that the genocide of the Armenians is still denied to this day? Why would such a man be still earthbound and why does he mourn so? He predicted World War II—does he mourn because of the future he sees in store for our country?

George Clemenceau, the prime minister of France, said of Wilson in 1919, "He thinks he is another Jesus Christ come upon the earth to reform men." If Wilson had succeeded, would not the world have been better for it? There would not have been a second world war and much of the chaos that ensued in the Middle East might have been avoided. If he had been allowed to do what he knew needed to be done, would his ghost linger in sorrow in the house where he spent his last sorrowful days?

Wilson once said, "It is not men that interest or disturb me primarily; it is ideas. Ideas live; men die." Wilson was a man of high ideals and staunch Presbyterian faith, and yet he still haunts the house he died in, unable to accept the fact he could not save the world. He had every right to be frightened of some people's ideas—the whole world had.

That best portion of a good man's life…his little, nameless unremembered acts of kindness.

William Wordsworth

EPILOGUE

I t is easy to get lost in the shadows behind the back steps; where ghosts lurk there are stories of the past. The Ghost of Christmas Past in Dickens's *A Christmas Carol* said to Scrooge, "I told you these were shadows of the things that have been. That they are what they are, do not blame me." Dickens knew ghosts well, and used them to show change and expose wrongdoings. His Ghost of Christmas Present says, "There are some upon this earth of ours, who lay claim to know us, and who do their deeds of passion, pride, ill-will, hatred, envy, bigotry, and selfishness in our name, who are as strange to us all our kith and kin, as if they had never lived. Remember that, and charge their doings on themselves not us." It is impossible not to apply much of this tale to the shadows that roam about in the most powerful city in the world. His lessons apply as much to the District of Columbia today as they did when it became the capital city. There are reasons that there are ghosts and spirits and it is the actions or inactions of human kind that cause them. It is the deeds and interactions of people that make the difference. The choices they made in life and the road they journeyed on affects the next journey when the corpse is only food for creepy crawlies. That we cannot prove that any of these ghostly sightings are real or if they were fabricated for various reasons is not important. What we are fortunate to have is a wealth of stories to entertain us, to make us ponder and to give us faith and hope. Those that believe in the supernatural see one way, especially those who have experienced it firsthand, and those who deny it will never agree with them or think them quite normal and sane. Everyone knows the earth is flat!

So much of what is termed as the paranormal has been sensationalized over the years and as so little is known about ghosts, spirits and death, it is very difficult to separate the urban legends from those that truly occurred. Human nature must also be taken into account, as memory, exaggeration and inexactitudes can alter the facts. The paranormal is not a science where the same test repeated over and over has the same results. Add a tea bag to water and you get tea but if every time you add a different type of tea and a different amount, the tea will never taste the same. Ghosts do not obviously abide by our laws, rules and regulations. They are not Pavlov's dogs, thus nothing about them is predictable. Ghosts are very much like ocean waves, their size and frequency dictated by themselves not by our standards. It has been said that space is the last frontier, but that is because so little serious research and experimentation has been done on the paranormal. We expect too much and give too little. You do not purchase a Tiffany vase at a discount store and yet there are those that will say they did or those who will be angry they didn't and do everything in their power to discredit with malice and forethought. The fact that I truly believe in the "supernatural" and have repeatedly had personal proof about its existence is not sufficient to make others, some of whom definitely don't want to believe, believe. One must be open to the experiences of the paranormal or nothing will ever happen, and even then there is no guarantee that anything will happen, let alone that it will be what we desire. One cannot guarantee that in a poker game you will be dealt all the aces.

Washington's ghosts are many and have their own agendas. Being in the right place at the right time and having an open, unbiased, logical mind are all important factors to witnessing these remaining souls. I'm sure there have been residents of the White House who are quite happy to share the building with those who have died but then there must be those who find it very uncomfortable. Perhaps it is time these stories are formally documented. No one is asking for Mr. Lincoln's fingerprints but the appearances and stories should be noted. There is more than one story that needs to be told and heard!

The Lincoln conspiracies have had scholars disagreeing for over a century and there doesn't seem to be any let up or lessening of interest in the subject. The spiritualist connection needs to be researched more, as do Secretary of War Stanton and the Knights of the Golden Circle. Official papers need to be opened so that much-needed pieces to the puzzle can be placed where they belong. Have these papers and documents been locked away in some shadowy tomb of a vault or have they been intentionally destroyed? Where do myth and conjecture meld with the facts? There are so many discrepancies and so many acts that reek of conspiracy, with the passage of so much time only the opening of official documents can fill in the much needed puzzle pieces.

Epilogue

There are hundreds of ghost tales from and about Washington that should have been included here except that it is too easy to get caught up in the White House and the Lincoln haunting. The old saying that one thing leads to another is true here. William Henry Harrison died of pneumonia one month after he became president of the United States in 1841. Supposedly a Shawnee Indian shaman placed a curse upon him and his house because of the defeat that he had inflicted upon the Shawnee in the battle of Tippecanoe in 1811. After that, every twenty years something happened to a president. Assuming that the house spoken of was the White House it only seems natural that the head of the house, the Great White Father, should be the one to die. In ancient times there was a saying and a custom, "The King must die." It is the tradition of the ritual scapegoat which we celebrate by killing off Father Time every New Year's Eve at midnight and placing on the throne, or in his job, the new baby who has all the powers of the old man he is replacing. There is not a beginning or an end but, like the great Worm (Orm-dragon) Ourberos, the symbol of the universe and eternity, who swallows his own tail, there is only a circle. Mankind has been debating the life-death cycle and immortality since way before Pharaoh Seti I of Egypt. This may be a great debate for theologians but the why and wherefore of ghosts is much more interesting. Imagine reading a great whodunit and when you get to the last page it is missing or you are told it was never written and you may solve it and present it as you would.

There is a very definite reason that the "fool" is the most powerful card in the Tarot Deck. The fool dares, the fool is inquisitive but logical, and the fool perseveres or dies trying. The fool is innovative and hunts wisdom and knowledge. The fool is the inventor, the creator, the investigator, the innovator and above all, regardless of the consequences, does what needs to be and should be done. The fool is wisdom itself and the banner barer of civilization. One can pervert a word but not a concept. Ideas live on long after we the living forget who said what or why.

> *"Farewell! The leaf-strown earth enfolds*
> *Our stay, our pride, our hopes, our fears,*
> *And Autumn's golden sun beholds*
> *A nation bowed, a world in tears."*

Oliver Wendell Homes

Whether you believe in ghosts or not, or even in the afterlife, you cannot sweep away the sightings as if they were ephemeral cobwebs or a bit of dust, as most of those people who have experienced and seen them are not

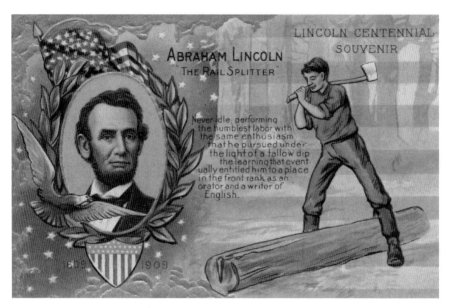

The centennial of Lincoln's assassination produced hundreds of postcards honoring the martyred president. Companies like Nash Publishing began churning out cards the year before showing Lincoln in every possible stage of his life. The cards are highly collectible today.

Just as this Civil War soldier contemplated the serene and tranquil Potomac so did Lincoln. The moments of quiet and peace that precede the storm are times for reflection. Knowing the horrors of war to come meant that all was not quiet on the Potomac and the hearts of many were stirred, saddened and frightened.

the types that would willingly involve themselves in paranormal encounters or make up stories about them. Most people are afraid to discuss their experiences lest people think they are lying or not quite right in the head. Those of us who are blessed with the power to see and want to use it are a minority and seldom have the opportunity to progress beyond the casual; but then it is said that fools rush in where angels fear to tread.

Then again there are those who actively dislike the entire notion of the paranormal and will go to any lengths to disprove and ridicule those who do actively accept it. Poor Nancy Reagan was treated as a madwoman because she, as many people before and since, was open and intelligent enough to want to seek answers and open vistas. This doesn't mean you believe everything you hear; it only means you keep an open mind and are receptive to any psychic experiences that you are privileged to encounter. Doors are to be opened as well as closed.

It is to be remembered that what *is* can be altered. As things stand now, such and such should or will happen, but if there are alterations everything changes. Lincoln understood this and wanted information so that he could change coming events. Options, the ability to make decisions, especially wise ones, can change everything. Imagine if Churchill had been given his way and Hitler was assassinated.

There are barriers between worlds and there are beings, both alive and spirit, which can breech them. Perhaps Abraham Lincoln is one.

BIBLIOGRAPHY

A ll books listed are from the Castle Halloween Museum, Betty Russell Memorial Library. All postcards and pictures are from the author's collection or the inventory of Chris Russell and the Halloween Queen™ Antiques.

Alexander, John. *Ghosts: Washington Revisited*. Atglen, PA: Schiffer Publishing, 1998.

———. *Ghosts: Washington's Most Famous Ghost Stories*. Arlington, VA: The Washington Book Trading Co., 1988.

Ayres, Alex, ed. *The Wit and Wisdom of Mark Twain*. New York: Harper & Row, 1987.

Balakian, Peter. *The Burning Tigris*. New York: Harper Collins, 2003.

Ballou, Adin. *Spirit Manifestations*. Bella Marsh Publishing, 1852.

Blavatsky, H.P. *The Secret Doctrine*, 3 vols. Pasadena, CA: The Theosophical University Press, 1928.

Cannon, Poppy, and Patricia Brooks. *The President's Cookbook*. New York: Funk & Wagnalls, 1968.

Carpenter, Liz. *Ruffles and Flourishes*. New York: Doubleday, 1970.

Conwell, Russell H. *The Life, Speeches and Public Services of James A. Garfield*. Portland, ME: Stinson & Co.,1881.

Bibliography

Cunliffe, Marcus. *George Washington: Man and Monument*. New York: Mentor Books, 1958.

DeGregorio, William. *The Complete Book of U.S. Presidents*. New York: Wing Books, 1993.

DeLorme, Maureen. *Mourning Art and Jewelry*. Atglen, PA: Schiffer Publishing, 2004.

Dickens, Charles. *A Christmas Carol*. New York: George Rutledge & Sons, 1887.

————. *Dombey and Son*. Cambridge edition in two volumes, 1882.

Edmonds, John W., and George T. Dexter, MD. *Spiritualism*, 2 vols. New York: Partridge & Brittan, 1853.

Gary, Ralph. *Following in Lincoln's Footsteps*. New York: Carroll and Graf Publishers, 2001.

Hare, Robert, MD. *Spirit Manifestations* New York: Partridge & Brittan, 1855.

Harpers Weekly, 1850s–1890s.

Leonardi, Dell. *The Reincarnation of John Wilkes Booth*. New York: Devin-Adair Co. Publishing, 1975.

Mayer, Henry. *All On Fire*. New York: St. Martin Griffin Publishers, 1998.

McCullough, David. *John Adams* New York: Simon & Schuster, 2001.

Page, Marian. *Historic Houses Restored and Preserved*. New York: Whitney Library of Design, 1976.

Reynolds, James. *Ghosts in American Houses*. New York: Bonanza Books, 1955.

Russell, Francis. *Adams: an American Dynasty*. Edison, NJ: Castle Books, 2005.

Schneider, Stuart. *Collecting Lincoln With Values*. Atglen, PA: Schiffer Publishing Co., 1997.

Bibliography

Shirley, David. *Thomas Nast: Cartoonist and Illustrator*. London: Franklin Watts Publishing, 1998.

Stapen, Candyce H., PhD. *Blue Guide Washington, D.C.* London: Somerset Books, 2000.

Taylor, L.B., Jr. *Civil War Ghosts of Virginia*. Lynchburg, VA: Progress Printing, 1995.

————. *The Ghosts of Virginia*, vol. 2. Virginia Ghosts, 1994.

United States Capitol Historical Society. "We, the People." 1963.

Whitman, Walt. *Leaves of Grass*. New York: Doubleday, Doran & Co., Inc., 1940.

Wills, Gary. *James Madison*. New York: Times Books, 2002.

About the Author

Pamela Apkarian-Russell is curator at Castle Halloween Museum in Benwood, West Virginia. The Halloween Queen ™ is her registered trademark. She is the author of nine books on Halloween, antiques, social history and the paranormal. Having made her living as an antiques dealer full time for thirty-five years, she writes extensively for antique trade journals, gives lectures and has appeared on television shows like "Martha Stewart" and "Collectors Lot" (which airs in the UK), as well as on the radio, speaking about antiques and Halloween memorabilia and the paranormal. Her short stories and ghost stories have appeared in both magazines and books. Pamela has not only written audio plays like "1921, the Christmas Letter," but has also acted in radio-broadcasted plays.

She resides with her husband, Christopher James Russell, and their cat, Bahron Mahrchoom the Magnificent. Their antique shop is known as Chris Russell & The Halloween Queen™. The shop, housed in the same building as the museum, specializes in postcards, ephemera, holiday items and folk art. To find out more about Castle Halloween Museum, visit www.castlehalloween.com.